SOOTHING SIPPING

Most people have heard of chamomile and spearmint and sassafras as healthful alternatives to orange pekoe. But did you know that from earliest history, people have used

- **basil and borage for a boost**
- **angelica for the flu**
- **wild strawberry to strengthen pelvic areas**
- **jasmine as an aphrodisiac**
- **ginger for digestion**

and at least sixty other plants from which to make tea that can heal and refresh? Noted herbalist and naturopath, author of three other successful books, Dorothy Hall is a reliable guide; she shares her knowledge of each herb's qualities, benefits—and some very important cautions.

If you want to simplify health maintenance or recuperation and give yourself a treat besides, here's an invitation to a tea-tasting that could become a life-long and life-prolonging adventure!

Other Keats Books of Relevant Interest

Bonnie Fisher's Way With Herbs Cookbook
by Bonnie Fisher

Choosing, Planting and Cultivating Herbs
by Philippa Back

Eat the Weeds
by Ben Charles Harris

Ginseng
by Ben Charles Harris

Growing Herbs as Aromatics
by Roy Genders

Guide to Medicinal Plants
by Paul Schauenberg and Ferdinand Paris

Herbs, Health and Astrology
by Leon Petulengro

How to Make Your Own Herbal Cosmetics
by Liz Sanderson

Making Things with Herbs
by Elizabeth Walker

Minnie Muenscher's Herb Cookbook
with woodcuts by Elfriede Abbe

Secrets of Natural Beauty
by Virginia Castleton

What Herbs Are All About
by Jack Joseph Challem and Renate Lewin-Challem

The Herb Tea Book

Dorothy Hall

Foreword by
David A. Phillips, Ph.D.

Illustrated with drawings
by Violette Niestle

Keats Publishing, Inc. New Canaan, Connecticut

The Herb Tea Book is not intended as medical advice. Its intention is solely informational and educational. Please consult a medical or health professional should the need for one be warranted. Neither the author nor the publishers have authorized the use of their names or the use of any of the material contained in this book in connection with the sale, promotion or advertising of any product or apparatus. Any such use is strictly unauthorized and in violation of the rights of Dorothy Hall and Keats Publishing, Inc.

THE HERB TEA BOOK

Pivot Health Edition published 1981 by Keats Publishing, Inc.

Copyright © 1980 by Dorothy Hall
Published by arrangement with The Pythagorean Press
Special contents © 1981 by Keats Publishing, Inc.

Library of Congress Catalog Card Number: 80-84436

Printed in the United States of America

Keats Publishing, Inc.
27 Pine Street, New Canaan, Connecticut 06840

CONTENTS

INTRODUCTION

HOW MANY different ideas on health are there? So many practitioners, even within the same nominal set of disciplines, espouse differing theories and principles. Perhaps there is a greater number of ideas on health than on religion (there are over 1200 variations of Christianity alone). Yet both fields of thought have much in common, especially the one central concept they share—their origin is traceable to Nature.

One of the most ancient aspects of health known is herbalism. Long before the apothecaries of old dispensed their medicinal and herbal drugs to relieve bodily illnesses, pristine people employed herbs in a diversity of applications with successful results. Modern people are astounded at how illness was cured without the aid of modern science. But it was; and only because people learned to observe Nature and to follow their intuition.

The modern trend has been to change Nature, so we think, to fit into our "scientific" concepts of how it should be. We employ complex diagnostic techniques and follow up with complicated chemical drugs as supposed solutions to personal health problems, problems which were ignored in their early and acute stage because we were too busy to take heed or because we did not know or use some simple kitchen remedies, believing them to be old-fashioned and quackish.

Very recent years have witnessed a considerable turn of direction of medical science. It now seeks to embrace the preventative disciplines, to take cognizance of early indications by the body that all might not be as it should be. And how often this occurs, while we are living at such a pace, with so much tension and anxiety, so many demands and emotional involvements.

By taking notice of our body we can save ourselves considerable inconvenience, expense and pain. Our body does not lie. If we learned to understand its language, to recognize its warning signals in their early and acute stage, our state of personal health would be greatly improved. And when we hear such warnings we must know what to do. This is where the ancient botanic science of herbalism comes into its own.

Most people understand enough about themselves to know when they should consult a professional practitioner about their diet or their body and its function. But few realize just how much independence they can achieve by using a basic selection of suitable herb teas to relieve those acute health problems.

It is for this reason that *The Herb Tea Book* has

been written. For decades there has been a need for a book which gives a clear, reasoned, uncomplicated set of guidelines on what herb teas to use, when and why. And who better to undertake such an important assignment than Australia's foremost authority on herbs and herbalism—Dorothy Hall.

It is doubtful if anyone else has a better understanding of the use of herbs in relation to the problems of today's Western civilization. She is certainly the leading exponent of herbalism in Australia. Her years of botanical training, which preceded her medical practice, gave Dorothy an unshakable foundation for her later studies and practice. She has consulted thousands of patients, written dozens of articles for magazines and journals and has written books on natural health, iridology and herbs, bringing to over 100,000 the total number of books in print under her enlightened authorship.

One of the secrets of Dorothy's success is her practical, down-to-earth, friendly approach to health and her patients. She is a lady who practices what she believes. This becomes readily evident to the reader of her books, and is especially apparent in this book.

Like any top nutritionist, Dorothy recognizes that the most important aspect of diet is enjoyment, so she pays particular attention to the flavor picture of herb teas, guiding her readers through a tea-tasting session such as has not appeared in any herb tea book previously.

Nothing of importance or interest is omitted from this book. It is indeed a most important addition to one's collection of books on health and nutrition.

DAVID A. PHILLIPS, PhD, ND

The Herb Tea Book

WHY DRINK HERB TEAS?

THERE SEEMS to be no valid reason for restricting our consumption of hot beverages to two plant sources. In many households a cup of tea or a cup of coffee are the only choices available when a hot drink is required.

How limiting this is! There are many plants which have been used in hot beverages, and not to investigate their uses in maintaining health and in simple disease prevention seems to be narrow and restricting.

In Europe, the Middle East and many of the more primitive communities, the range of plants to choose from in making a cuppa is more varied. Recorded information about various plants used in the making of teas has been proven beneficial to the human body by many thousands of years of use. How many pharmaceutical drug companies can claim such a period of testing?

There is, therefore, a need to have facts made available on the simple use of herbal plants in tea form. It is then up to each individual to decide which herb teas benefit and comfort them. One person's herb tea may be distasteful to another, but more exposure to trying the various teas and discovering those most suitable is needed. It is my wish that the information in this book will make you more venturesome in testing and trying.

Most herb teas are made from dried plant materials. It becomes too difficult to always make herb teas from the fresh source, even if one has fresh herbs available in the backyard all year round. Equally limiting, many of the teas which are useful are not easily grown, preferring the more alkaline soils of Europe or the more mineral-rich soils of other parts of the world. Many soils are deficient in nutrients needed by herbs to maintain their chemical balance during growth. For instance, some of the minerals necessary for the leaf growth of many plants are only minimally available in sandstone regions. Soil variations can be quite extreme, resulting in fresh herbs with such widely varying physiological effects that you would swear that botanically they were not the same.

Thus, in one country, teas made from fresh herbs can be quite different in content to those brewed in countries where the herbs grow naturally in more suitable soil conditions. Many of the reported "odd" results obtained when making herb teas from fresh sources are directly attributable to these soil and climatic differences. It is much wiser to obtain herbs dried professionally in the countries where they grow best. Such dried material, correctly packaged to maintain its freshness, is often better for tea-making than the fresh plants.

Ease of use is another important factor for today's busy people. I find that people prefer to drink herb tea if it is readily available from a jar in the kitchen rather than if they have to take five steps outside the back door to harvest the fresh plant!

The method of making herb teas is much the same for all varieties, but teas made from *bark* and plant *roots* need a little longer to brew. Generally, bark and root teas are higher in *mineral* content, especially heavy minerals such as iron and copper. This property demands extra brewing time for maximum extraction of flavor and nutrients. A general rule to apply, if your herb tea is made from these parts of the plant, is to allow it to stand in the pot for five to ten minutes. You can often benefit from slightly reheating these teas before drinking them.

If your herb tea is made from the *leaves* of the plant it is better to brew it quickly and drink it piping hot, and in that way gain the maximum *vitamin* content.

Teas from *flowers* of plants fall in a middle area between these two extremes. They should be brewed for a few minutes more than leaf teas.

Now let us get down to the simple techniques of making herb tea. The general instructions are to take a teaspoon of the dried material for every cup of liquid needed, and a little extra for the pot—if you are making tea for a few people. Soak the herbs in water which is just off the boil for three to five minutes before drinking the tea.

If making just one cup of tea for yourself, you can use the good old-fashioned infusion method. Simply place the herbal material in your cup and pour the boiling water on it. The plant material will become saturated and sink slowly to the bottom of the cup during the initial minutes of brewing so that you need not sip mouthfuls of stalk and leaf fiber when drinking the tea.

The brew can be strained into another cup, but don't throw out the residue of your herb tea with the kitchen garbage. Return it to the soil, either via the compost heap or lightly dug into the topsoil. This way, many of the more stubborn-to-extract mineral contents remaining after brewing are returned for the benefit of other plants.

Many herb tea manufacturers are aware of customer resistance to some of the strange and wonderfully exotic tastes available from plants. For this reason they have blended many herbs together to form more palatable mixtures which, although still acting in the body according to their individual components, are vastly more attractive to the taste buds.

Such mind-tickling names as "Stockman's Brew," "Sleepy-time Tea," "Orange Mist," "Pelican Punch" and "Dreamtime" have come onto the market to pander a little to those folks who will not experience something new unless it is also easy and pleasant. Some of these blends are quite exquisite in flavor and many have spices added to highlight particular fragrances and tastes. It is sometimes possible to find herb tea available in single tea bags or in small sample packets, so that if you don't like a particular flavor or combination you need not be stuck with an enormous jar of it.

It is fun to try blending your own flavors, but keep the savory flavors together and sweet flavors separated if possible. One patient reported to me that she experienced great delight from a blend of fenugreek, chamomile and comfrey, with a pinch of pepper and a slice of lemon! Her palate must have been either jaded or dead if it could not recognize that these flavors were basically incompatible.

Experiment by mixing and matching herb teas according to either their sweetness or their pungency: but you will drown one with the other if you mix the two.

Add fresh material to your herb tea to give variation to its taste. A slice of lemon, a piece of orange peel, a pinch of cinnamon, even a smidgen of good vegetable salt or seasoning can be added to some teas to make each cup a different experience. One lady I know pours her lemongrass tea over a few raisins in the bottom of the cup. A busy executive takes his rosehips tea with a cinnamon stick. One of the worst herb tea combinations I have ever heard of was concocted by a gentleman who added a teaspoon of cooking salt to his fenugreek tea under the impression that he was improving its flavor! Instead, he produced curry-flavored sea-water. Be careful with your additives.

Become aware of the many taste experiences possible with herb teas. Do it *gradually*. Is your palate so deadened by the over-use of salt and sugar, then kicked back to life by black coffee, that the subtle differences of herb tea flavors are lost on you altogether?

Don't go overboard and buy sixteen different packets of herb tea. Pick a tea which appeals to you, then decide whether it is your "thing" or not.

Be especially prudent where caution is advised in the use of any of the teas in this book. You will certainly find it's best to start with a pleasant-tasting blend. Do not try to treat yourself for major illness—seek professional advice.

In my practice as a herbalist I treat patients with many therapeutic concentrations of plant material. I recommend the use of various extracts and tinctures, oils and ointments, to help them achieve a particular plateau of health. But when they ask me if they need to keep coming back now that they feel so good I explain that they can maintain this plateau with such simple substances as herb teas and dietary control. I advise the patient who had lost chronic sinusitis and is terrified of its return in winter to start in autumn on fenugreek tea. This particular program can mean that the sinusitis is simply and permanently out of the way.

The home use of herb tea as preventive medicine is a relatively untapped and vastly useful health measure. If you resent dependence upon expensive health care after illness has developed, take simple *preventive* measures in the home to maintain general good health. This will enable you to quickly balance those initial processes of illness so that, in many cases, they need not deteriorate into chronic ill health.

If it sounds like a return to grandma's day when strange brews with wonderfully exotic smells were prepared in the kitchen and doled out in wineglassful doses to protesting relatives, maybe it is. But in grandma's day home health care was better understood. It was much less intrusive than many of the more unsavory acute treatments of disease then available. Once a process of disease was past the home treatment stage, you were often as good as dead! Modern scientific medicine has made this situation less likely, but I feel that the relatively untapped areas of home prevention and simple health care have fallen into disuse, resulting in over-dependence on medical care to treat major disease. How nice to become a little more self-sufficient in maintaining one's health, and in such a simple, pleasant and non-costly way!

So start your herb tea adventure soon. Explore the delights of flavor and fragrance, experience changes which you might have thought impossible. Never believe for a moment that the average householder is qualified or trained to correct major disease by a cup of this and a cup of that. But simpler symptoms, readily understood and easily predictable, can be treated at home by the wise use of herb teas. If the process of illness is not halted this way, I strongly recommend that you seek professional attention.

Sensible use of herb tea offers social and healthy enjoyment. Do not overuse or abuse herb tea drinking—it is intended to be an occasional pleasure, not an endless habit. Remember, even the healthiest habits demand the exercise of moderation.

Have fun with your taste buds! Try this, try that; open up a whole new approach to drinking pleasure and to maintaining health and well-being.

ALPHABETICAL LISTING
OF HERBS

Chamomile

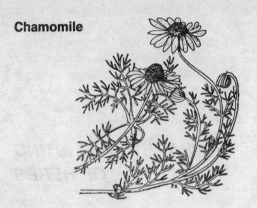

ALFALFA

(Medicago sativa)

Probably best known by its American name, alfalfa ("lucerne" to the British) is an extremely deep-rooted legume. It has pretty, purple flowers and a habit of growth which draws nitrogen from the soil, storing it in nodules on the stem.

Any plant with this ability has an alkalizing effect when taken into the body. Thus alfalfa tea can be one of the best choices for people with hyper-acid stomachs. People with arthritic acid conditions in the joints and people who have recently given up meat often find their stomachs produce too much acid. If they are still eating fish they could again find too much gastric acid is being produced. Alfalfa tea can rearrange this balance a little so that gastric acid production drops to suit a vegetarian diet.

Alfalfa as a general tea should be used in countries where a high proportion of carbohydrate prevails in the diet. If you enjoy eating pasta, if you often eat bread, or if you are fond of the "good" complex carbohydrates, such as buckwheat, rice and whole wheat (even if you are having muesli every morning), you can find that your gastric acidity is a little higher than it should be. Alfalfa tea is an excellent acid balancer. This tea also helps to produce saliva which provides a benefit for the digestion by initiating the early breakdown of starches in the mouth.

Alfalfa contains nine amino acids similar to those contained in animal protein. Thus, it can help to break down hard-to-digest protein residues from animal sources. For this reason it is also beneficial for folk with particular protein allergies. These include the sinus and hay fever sufferers as well as those who break out in a rash when they drink milk or eat eggs, strawberries, prawns or any other substance which produces uncomfortable allergic reactions. These people are probably deficient in one or more amino acids needed to properly digest these foods. Alfalfa can provide home help for a person with such a history of food allergies. It can also benefit children who are allergic to particular kinds of foods.

Alfalfa tea can be mixed with mint to give it a much more sparkling flavor. You will find children rather enjoy the mint taste. They can be started on alfalfa tea quite early if they have difficulty with particular foods.

The dried leaves and flowers of the plant are used to make alfalfa tea. Being such a deep-rooted plant, alfalfa draws minerals from the subsoil and its tea is high in alkalizing salts, especially sodium phosphate. It also contains vitamins A, B and C although, as with any herb tea, the content of these nutrients depends significantly on the care with which the plant was dried.

Alfalfa tends to support enzyme activity, so you can think of it as a digestive tea. Its combination with peppermint results in a most beneficial digestive aid. The best time to drink it is between meals, when you stop work to have a cup of something hot. Drink alfalfa tea if your stomach is upset from the previous meal. As a cold tea it can be added to fruit cups in the summer. Mix it with a little chopped mint and some orange rind or lemon peel to use as a cold additive to juices. Alfalfa is a flavor which mixes well with fruit or vegetable juice.

ANGELICA

(Angelica officinalis or Angelica archangelica)

This herb is occasionally found in mixtures and blends of herb teas. Its mild and rather pleasantly sweet taste (like celery flavored with sugar) can also make it a very pleasant tea for children. Angelica can be used therapeutically to make the patient feel better during any cold, virus or influenza-type illness. Historically, it was often given to prevent such an illness becoming a chronic, long-term health hazard for the patient.

Angelica, which could be classed as a green vegetable, grows in many temperate parts of the world. Its leaves are large and profuse and the name derives from the supposition that the leaves possessed angelic healing properties. The upper stems of the plant can be candied and used as a confection. It is a pleasantly-flavored tea which can be mixed with any other sweet-tasting beverage.

Its contents are quite remarkable: Angelica contains about 5 percent copper salts. It also contains carotene, providing the liver with the raw material from which vitamin A is made. Angelica possesses some plant steroids, thereby helping to support processes of immunity in the body. Another of its contents is valerianic acid, helpful in calming the nerves. Pectin, an enzyme essential for the stomach's easy digestion of food, is also present. This helps angelica to become a mild antispasmodic and digestive aid. Because of these factors, angelica can be truly called a broad general tonic.

ANISEED

(Pimpinella anisum)

Most people know and like the flavor of aniseed, but we occasionally find some who think it repugnant. If this is the case, it means that your body does not require anethol, aniseed's most prominent ingredient. Anethol is an oil found in the seeds and leaves of the plant (a small flowering annual). It works within the pancreas to help the digestive processes connected with pancreatic enzymes.

Aniseed tea can be prepared by crushing the anise seeds with a blunt instrument, such as the end of a wooden spoon (you could even use a kitchen grinder), pouring on boiling water and allowing to stand for at least five minutes. The tea can then be drunk hot or cool.

Aniseed tea is particularly refreshing when you are experiencing the throbbing miseries of a head cold—when nostrils are blocked, the throat is catarrhal and clogged, breathing is difficult and upper sinuses are aching. It should be taken three or four times a day when the cold is at its worst.

Most small children like the flavor of aniseed and will drink the tea with honey or some lemon juice. When other means of removing cold and flu symptoms may be too unpleasant or difficult, aniseed tea can be an excellent decongestant for children.

BARLEY

(Hordeum vulgare)

Barley as a tea? Yes, certainly! The process of boiling barley grains until they are soft and then straining the thick liquid from the soggy remains, produces a substance which can be called tea.

Before serving, flavor the thick barley liquid with a little lemon juice or cinnamon, or mix with a fresh fruit juice to thin it a little.

It is such a valuable panacea for the modern scourge of so many females—cystitis—that I feel it should be included as an important household remedy. Barley tea should be taken in half to cupful doses during painful urgency and frequency of urination in a cystitis attack. It can soothe the irritated bladder linings and bring symptomatic comfort quickly. Meanwhile, professional advice should be sought to discover and correct the *cause* of the cystitis.

Even for those other present day curses of monilia and trichomonis, barley tea can be a boon while the symptoms are troublesome.

BASIL

(Ocymum basilicum)
& BORAGE

(Borago officinalis)

These two pleasant-tasting herbs have quite

marked cooling and tonic effects. Together they make an ideal "housewife's tea" to remedy that mid-morning slump which occurs after the family has gone to work and school, the house has been tidied and the lady of the house feels the need for a general pick-me-up. The powerful and fast-acting basil balances the slower and more cooling borage to rapidly stimulate you, then maintain you at that improved level.

Basil is an annual plant found in most tropical regions. It can be easily cultivated as a kitchen herb. Many people fail to pick it during its growth period, only to find at the end of the season that the basil is yellow, woody, dying off and rather useless as a household plant.

Borage does not suffer from this problem. If you have ever grown borage you know that you will never get rid of it from your garden. It will self-sow and distribute its little seedlings for many yards around, even onto your neighbor's property. There will be no shortage of borage leaves to mix with the basil leaves for your household tea.

The therapeutic properties of both plants are remarkably reduced after the leaves have been dried. Tea prepared from the dried ingredients has a less noticeable effect than that made from the living plants.

The basil half of this mixture is a general pick-me-up tonic and stimulant for the tissues of the brain. It clears the head and can help remove that pressure feeling (which later in the day can produce a "pressure" headache and feeling of nausea).

Borage works through the kidneys, the skin and the heart to support energy by maintaining good circulation through these organs. A noticeable boost in energy is often the first feeling after a cup of basil and borage tea. This effect can last for the remainder of the day. Thus the tea is better taken as a mid-morning beverage than at night, when you really don't want to produce a surge of energy, you just want to go to sleep! So try basil and borage as your morning cuppa.

BILBERRY

(Vaccinium myrtillus)

All the berry fruits contain iron, copper, vitamin C and the vitamins known as the bioflavonoids. This combination, found in all ripe berries, works through the bloodstream—through the major and minor circulation to all organs of the body. Bilberries are bluish in color and are the fruits of a perennial shrub which does best in sandy soils and temperate climates.

Bilberry tea is made from the dried berries after they have ripened to the point where their vitamin and mineral content is highest. It has a pleasant taste and can be a beneficial drink for elderly people with circulation problems. It can also be beneficial as a post-operative tea to support the circulation after interference with its processes during surgery.

Lemon rind blends very nicely with bilberry-fruit tea. Some people might feel the flavor of bilberry is too bland, in which case the lemon will add a pleasant tanginess. Many people have enjoyed a fruit punch made on a base of bilberry tea: to a large bowl, add your choice of diced fruits and/or juices, plus sprigs of fresh spearmint, some apple cider and lemon juice; then mix in cold bilberry tea to give color and depth of flavor.

BLACK CURRANT

(Ribes nigrum or ribes americanum)

As a household cool tea in the summer and a hot beverage in colder weather, black currant is a delightfully versatile drink. As with all berry-originating herb teas, black currant is a valuable source of vitamin C, accompanied by the bioflavonoids (vitamin P), making for the best assimilation of both. If the tea is made without the inclusion of any berries, at least try to have some of the leaf stems included, for they provide some of the vitamin and mineral contents of the berries themselves.

Black currant tea is usually made only from the leaves of the bush, when obtained commercially. But many people prefer to prepare their own black currant tea after collecting and drying the leaves and stems of the bushes they have cultivated in their garden or orchard. In this manner, they obtain those extra nutrients and the unparalleled satisfaction of doing the whole thing themselves.

The black currant bush is an attractive and useful addition to any home garden and can be a valuable commercial asset to any orchard. It generally grows to a height of up to seven feet, producing a mantle of pale green flowers in the springtime as a prelude to fruiting in the summer. Its fruits are very small, delicious eaten fresh or dried, but they can cause diarrhea if taken in excess, whereas the tea will not.

In addition to the nutrients already mentioned, folic acid (an important member of the B-group of vitamins), is present in both leaves and fruit. Its value in the leaves provides further contribution to the usefulness of this herb tea and the pleasures it can create as a social drink. As a pleasant stimulus to the taste buds, black currant tea can be enjoyed by every member of the family. It mixes well with other flavors, such as rose hips, lemon verbena or lemon grass. It can also be effectively used as a base for delicious fruit punches.

BLUEBERRY

(Gaylussacia frondoas)

Almost as American as apple pie is the deep

indigo hue and the succulent sweetness of the blueberry. Softer in texture than most other berries, it can be very easily digested and is very easily cultivated, being found almost everywhere in the U.S.A.

Therapeutic properties of the blueberry bush are similar to most other berry varieties, the leaves of which are utilized for herb tea brewing. Nutritional properties include vitamin C, iron and copper, accompanied by the bioflavonoids and folic acid.

Blueberry leaf tea makes a very pleasant pre-meal or social beverage. It can be served hot in winter or cool in the warmer weather. Either way, it is easy to prepare and enjoyable to drink.

BOLDO

(Pemeus boldus)

A comparative newcomer in herb tea lists, boldo can be found added to teas blended together for slimming diets. The plant is a small shrubby tree, a native of Chile, with strong-smelling leathery leaves and unpleasant-tasting yellow-green fruits.

Its function in the body is to work through the "yellow" system—the liver, gall bladder and pancreas—and also through the digestive tract. It is known to aid digestion by stimulating these organs and, for some people, body weight appears to drop on drinking boldo tea regularly. However, if the excess weight is coming from some cause other than sluggish digestion, boldo tea might not be as effective as the label could have you believe. It certainly stimulates gastric acid production and therefore enables food to be digested more completely.

BURDOCK ROOT

(Arctium lappa)

This is a perennial plant which enjoys growing wild in temperate climates. From the root of Burdock comes a highly medicinal tea. I hesitate to recommend the general use of this tea, for its silica and iron compounds are anything but gentle. An overload of these chemicals can induce uncomfortable elimination symptoms through the skin, soft tissues and bowels, increased urination, stronger sweat and abdominal discomfort. But the story is not all bad . . .

The herb tea, brewed from dried root pieces of the burdock plant, offers important therapeutic properties. It can be of appreciable benefit to sufferers of sciatica and the type of rheumatoid arthritis which has dry, hot joints creating sharp pain on movement. Its silica salts help burdock root tea break up crystals of uric acid and promote its fluid excretion through the kidneys and bowels as well as via the skin's perspiration. Its use should be employed sparingly, even for such rheumatic sufferers. A medium-strength cup should be adequate each second or third day, increasing the intake only if under professional guidance. A cup each day is almost certainly too much.

Burdock root tea contains bitter resins, one of which is the alkaloid lappine. It is responsible for the strong purging effect if taken in excess. Another ingredient, potassium nitrate, can stimulate heart function for rheumatic sufferers. But ingredients can be not only uncomfortable, but downright dangerous if the drink is taken in excess. That bitter taste should be your warning. Successful use of herb teas often depends on the accuracy of your information. They are not all the same. Care and proper guidance should always be employed.

CATNIP

(Nepeta cataria)

Catnip is a garden herb, a member of the mint family which has grown wild in England for centuries. This shrub is perennial and much old information about it seems to be somewhat misleading as to its relationship to cats. Some cats will walk past catnip without so much as a flicker of interest. Others will rush up to it, roll around in it and become wildly excited by the smell from either the leaves or the roots. Other cats will be distressed and infuriated by the plant and endeavor to remove it from the garden by scratching it out.

Likewise, catnip tea will produce a variety of reactions among humans. You may find that it either calms you and makes you feel delightfully relaxed, or can upset you a little and produce a mild depressive effect. This latter property of the plant makes its use as a tranquillizing tea debatable and somewhat chancy. You must try it yourself to find out which way it affects you. However, it often works as a mild sedative to calm down those hyperactive, energetic moods most healthy children seem to experience all day and far too long into the evening hours.

Catnip tea is brewed from the dried leaves of the plant. It has a taste one can only describe as bitter-sweet.

CELERY SEED

(Apium graveolens)

This tea must be used with extreme care. The seeds of celery contain such powerful mineral combinations that too much celery seed tea can upset the body's mineral balance. This tea should definitely be recorded as "medicinal only" because its action in the body is indeed a strong one.

Celery seed contains potassium and phosphorus compounds of a type which stimulate kidney function and the excretion of uric acid. These same mineral compounds are used in healthy muscle function. Thus, the combination of these chemicals tends to reduce muscular pain, spasm and cramps, especially in some arthritic conditions.

High in sulphur compounds, celery seed tea is alterative in its action through the bloodstream and the bowels. It also contains many iron salts to help oxidize and burn out rubbish. Two significant minerals in celery seed tea are silica and sodium. These two work nicely together to blast out acid residues from tissues and from general body structures. Magnesium, also found in this tea, contains salts which support physical nerve function.

It can be occasionally used by diabetics because it tends to be compatible with pancreas function and will not raise or lower blood sugar levels.

Vitamins A, B-complex and C are present in celery seed tea, although there is more vitamin C to be found in the leaves of the plant.

Celery seed is often blended with juniper berries. This combination gives an extremely sharp stimulus to kidney function. The added juniper stimulates renal arteries and the renal pelvis. Thus, for arthritic and rheumatic sufferers, symptomatic treatment can regularly include celery seed tea.

The level at which this tea is tolerated varies from individual to individual. A good dose to commence with is a cup each day made from a teaspoon of the ground, pulverized or crushed seeds. Celery seed tea can be made in advance and added in small quantities to soups and stews if the flavor is enjoyed or if the therapeutic properties are desired. Prepared in this way it can be equally useful, in small amounts on a daily basis, for an arthritic or rheumatic person.

CHAMOMILE

(Anthemis nobilis)

English Chamomile

(Matricaria chamomilla)

German Chamomile

This is one of the most useful teas for everyone, from the youngest child to the oldest grandparent. Chamomile tea is so well known in Europe and was so extensively used as an everyday beverage two or three generations ago that its relative lack of use today is surprising.

The part of the chamomile plant used is the golden conical center of each of the small daisy-like flowers of both varieties of the plant, together with a few of the petals surrounding this central cone. German chamomile has a little more volatile oil available than the English variety, but the English flowers can be effectively blended with it. This is often done in commercial preparations.

[27]

The habit of growth of each plant is quite different. The English chamomile is a perennial creeper, often used as a lawn in Europe, with tiny daisy-like flowers. It needs a humid, cool climate in which to grow best. The German variety is a more hardy annual and needs to be resown every year. Its feathery leaves have a grey tinge and its upright habit of growth is botanically quite different from the English variety.

The unusual flavor of chamomile tea intrigues many people. It could be described as a silky smooth blend of apples and cloves, with the delightful aroma of an arrangement of sweet spring flowers.

Most people, especially children, enjoy the flavor of chamomile tea. This is indeed fortunate because chamomile tea is excellent as a general herb tea for children, those who are small and teething as well as older ones who are having difficulty with starting school and are tense, nervous and highly strung. Chamomile tea is especially beneficial for hyperactive children, its effect being to calm their nervous activity and assist them to gain better control of it, certainly not to *stop* it. As a pre-bed drink for children, especially if they have engaged in stimulating activities after dinner, chamomile tea can aid in securing a good night's sleep—and this contributes to a better night's sleep for the parents!

For those self-same parents, it may be a good idea to try chamomile tea at night, especially after too much food, drink and good company have been enjoyed. Many people have complained to me that on getting into bed "a large lump seems to sit fair in the solar plexus." This is undigested food about to inhibit the relaxing sleep which that particular person invariably needs.

As a nightcap, a cup of chamomile tea is unbeatable. One of its best uses is for calming the vagus nerve (the tenth cranial nerve), which plays a large part in the digestive and respiratory processes. It is also extremely beneficial for relaxation of the muscular patterns around the head and face and in the calming of processes of overactive thought, when the head is busy and full of the past day's doings or the next day's problems.

Chamomile's effect on the vagus nerve is also beneficial for the stomach. This nerve ends near the base of the stomach and is involved in the digestive processes. Chamomile tea will provide it with enough calcium phosphate to aid the digestion, leaving still more calcium available for the nervous system, so that it can relax.

The nutritional and therapeutic contents of chamomile include the phosphates of calcium, magnesium and potassium—all of which play a large part in calming the physical, emotional and intellectual nerve centers of the body. This makes it a useful tea for relieving those cramping spasms some women—especially teenagers—experience at period time.

Chamomile tea is relaxing, but it is not a sedative. It is calming, but not addictive. It is pleasant-

THE HERB TEA BOOK

tasting, but does not need to be increased in quantity to stimulate the taste buds or produce the same overall effect.

Chamomile tea is an excellent aid to dispelling tension, to calming the muscular and nervous systems and to preparing the digestive tract for the evening meal. For this reason, chamomile tea is excellent for adults and children who suffer from "abdominal migraine"—those grabbing pains in the stomach which prevent them from eating when under any form of tension. It's also ideal for those overworked people who are so exhausted when they arrive home in the evening that the digestive tract is not fit to handle an evening meal. I have known many patients who like a cup of chamomile tea as soon as they arrive home in the evening; they spend the next hour before dinner quietly, feeling relaxed, comfortable and well able to digest their food.

You can add chamomile tea to cool bathwater in cases of severe sunburn. You can use it as a rinse if your hair is naturally fair and lacking lustre and brilliance. You can rub the slippery soft remains of the chamomile flowers through your hands and find that the smooth silkiness of chamomile acts as an emollient on the skin.

As you can see, chamomile is a useful herb tea and it is universally available in dried form. It is a shame not to use this herb often as a regular household remedy to help prevent the serious accumulation of nervous tension and digestive problems so characteristic of modern living. Most suppliers have it available in tea-bag form, encouraging its use in the office, for the mid-afternoon cuppa, especially after that rather tense, rather too heavy, rather indiscreetly-chosen business lunch. Chamomile tea is an absolute boon to those of us living a "civilized" existence.

CHICORY

(Cichorium intybus)

The root of chicory, chopped and dried, makes a passable stand-in for coffee. Many of the coffee substitutes on health food store shelves contain chicory root, as well as grains like rye, barley, buckwheat, and legumes such as soya beans.

When young, the chicory plant looks a bit like dandelion. As it grows, its green rosette of young leaves shoots up a tall candelabra-shaped flower spike with new, deep blue petals fading to white each day. The plant is grown as a fodder crop in many parts of the world, but its root is far more valuable for it contains starch and choline, important in the regulation of the liver's cholesterol metabolism. Chicory is also high in vitamin A (needed by the liver, eyes and skin) primarily in the form of carotene.

As chicory works so well through the liver, it is recommended for illnesses such as hepatitis, alcoholism and similar diseases of "civilized" living. Nothing is harder on one's liver than the combination of over-refined foods, over-indulgence in alcohol and smoking. People who are determined to keep (or unable to give up!) such patterns should drink herb teas of chicory root and dandelion to help their overloaded livers cope better.

Chicory leaves, when fresh, contribute a strangely bitter taste to a green salad. However, the leaves are usually not added to the tea.

CINNAMON

(Cinnamomum zylanicum)

A member of the huge laurel family of trees and shrubs, the cinnamon tree is native to the Middle East and parts of Central America, Asia and Africa. The powdered aromatic spice is extracted from the bark, not only of the cinnamon tree, but of many of those of the laurel family. Its unique flavor is characteristic of Lebanese vegetables, as well as of Indian curries. Its original use was as a preservative for meats which required lengthy periods of storage in hot climates.

As a herb tea, cinnamon is chosen more for its flavor than therapeutic properties. It is one of my favorite flavors, especially when added to other aromatic spice teas, such as hibiscus. It also mixes exceptionally well with berry teas and those with a lemon flavor.

Therapeutically, cinnamon tea is used by many people to help clear the brain and improve the thinking processes. It can be very beneficial to students when studying intensively prior to examination time. A drop of oil of cinnamon in a warm bath is known to have a similar effect, but care must be taken to use only one drop and to mix it well with the bath water, for cinnamon oil can be almost caustic in its pure, concentrated form.

CLOVES

(Caryophyllus aromaticus)

Cloves are a spice formed by the unopened, dried flower buds of an evergreen native to the tropical Spice Islands, probably originating in the Moluccas. They have been known and used from classical times for their preservative and anti-putrefaction effects on foods. Throughout the centuries before refrigeration, cloves were used as one of the preserving spices which arrested food decay, simultaneously conferring upon the food a delightfully new and spicy aroma and flavor.

For centuries, clove oil was used as an ingredient in embalming. It was also found to be useful in the household to gently anesthetize various types of nerve pain. The old household remedy of applying a drop of clove oil to an aching tooth is well known.

Cloves used as an additive to some of the spicier herb tea blends can have an amazingly gentle effect in soothing the gastric and intestinal mucosa (the linings of the stomach and intestines). They also tend to offer a neutralizing, counterirritant effect when cooked with foods which are acid or otherwise highly spiced. If your stomach is protesting against the last trip to the Indian Curry House, you should ensure that next time you select dishes with some form of cloves in the spice mixture added to the food. Or better yet, when you get home have a herb tea which contains cloves mixed with, say, ginger or cinnamon or even some mint leaves. Cloves mix best in herb tea blends which use a mild flavor base, such as alfalfa (which also adds to the antacid benefits), orange peel and rosehips (a fruit and spice effect) for a sparkling midday boost of energy.

A so-called nervous stomach can be made to feel quite relaxed after a cup of tea containing cloves. The prolonged use of clove tea might just send your stomach to sleep, and it may not know what it is eating if you over-indulge in other particularly powerful spices.

COLTSFOOT

(Tussilago farfara)

Coltsfoot does not grow naturally in sub-tropical or warm temperate climates, preferring the deciduous beech and oak forests of England, Europe and North America. An unusual little plant, it is a perennial and one of the first to appear on the forest floor in the early spring. Its stems resemble brown asparagus, and its bright, open-faced, yellow flowers cheer away the last cold days of winter.

People who smoke tobacco may use coltsfoot tea to offset some of the effects of the dreaded weed. It is better to give up smoking altogether, but if you are finding it difficult to do so (which means you can dismiss the thought of all those coal tar deposits in your lungs and irritated bronchial tubes), coltsfoot tea can help loosen some of the residues caused by heavy tobacco usage. You will realize this when you cough and splutter and remove a lot of mucus as you drink coltsfoot tea! You may be quite amazed at some of the rubbish that your chest has been accumulating while you have been smoking.

Coltsfoot tea is brewed from the leaves and flowers of the plant, which contain valuable iron in phosphate form. It also contains mucilage which is soothing and a gentle expectorant for the lungs and bronchial tree. It is high in natural sugars—providing energy for the muscles of the chest—and has quite a high organic acid content to help remove infection from traumatized respiratory areas. The small amount of tannin in coltsfoot also helps to tone and tighten mucous linings of the bronchial tree and of the lungs, which may be underactive after heavy tobacco usage or lack of adequate daily exercise.

The phosphates in coltsfoot tea are supported by calcium salts, so expectoration, coughing and elimination of rubbish from the bronchial tree and lungs should not cause damage. Calcium salts help to heal old scar tissue and irritated patches.

COMFREY

(Symphytum officinale)

Without wishing to join the technical arguments about comfrey or any of its supposedly dangerous ingredients, as a practicing herbalist for many years I have never found comfrey tea disadvantageous in any way, shape or form. I will leave the scientists and chemists to argue about possible toxic effects from the use (or abuse) of the plant, but in my own experience the contents of it are balanced and not toxic under normal conditions of usage.

Over-use of almost any substance can produce results which are less than balanced. But huge quantities of comfrey leaves would need to be ingested to induce a deleterious effect on the body, quantities far in excess of the body's normal digestive ability. Instead, a cup of comfrey tea can be taken as a pleasant, bland, rather haylike flavored insurance against various body disease processes.

Comfrey tea is known to be a safe drink and is not cumulative in its effects. I would suggest its use *occasionally* and also suggest that its *continued* use is not necessary. At times when there is body damage (surgery; accidents where scar tissue can be formed, like abrasions, cuts, fractures; even when there is severe interruption to body function by removal of an organ, or even amputation), comfrey is supportive to the processes of cell regeneration and normal tissue replacement.

Many people find comfrey to be a tea which needs some other flavor to support its rather musty taste. You can add mint, alfalfa or one of the more cheery-tasting herbs to make a very pleasant blend. Comfrey/mint is an excellent beverage for people who have a tendency towards arthritic conditions or gout because it helps to neutralize uric acid residues.

The nutritional and therapeutic contents of comfrey are variable, depending on the condition of the plant at the time of picking and the method by which it is dried. Chemical changes take place when comfrey is improperly dried. When purchasing comfrey tea, check the pack to ensure the contents are still *green*. Once the comfrey leaves have browned and oxidized their therapeutic contents can be quite different.

Allantoin is one important substance to be found in green comfrey leaves. Its value as a healing agent following body trauma is becoming more widely recognized. Scar tissue can be minimized when allantoin is applied and even the later tendency to adhesion formation can be reduced. This is just one of the therapeutic uses of comfrey tea.

Bear in mind that comfrey should *not* be used as an antiseptic. If the skin is damaged and open you should use a herbal antiseptic, such as Calendula, before applying comfrey leaves because the skin could heal too quickly, retaining any infection underneath.

Cosmetically, the soggy remains of the comfrey leaves can have many uses. Throw them in your bathwater for a beneficial skin care treatment while bathing. You can also sit in the sun with comfrey leaf soggily and greenly plastered all over your face for a simple inexpensive wrinkle-removing pack. Another important use is to dab the mucilaginous comfrey tea residues on sores or ulcerated areas, particularly around varicose ulcers, or saltwater ulcers.

Many patients with metabolic diseases—such as diabetes, celiac disease, anemia, even anorexia nervosa—can have comfrey tea prescribed by professionals as a part of their treatment. Using it as a strong therapeutic agent is most assuredly best left to professional practitioners who have studied comfrey's properties.

CORN SILK

(Zea Mays)

Whether you grow your own vegies or buy them from the markets, you probably throw away some of their most valuable parts. For instance, corn cobs usually have their protective covering unceremoniously discarded prior to cooking. But the tassled creamy silk from the cob can be chopped up and effectively used as a herb tea.

Corn silk tea can be easily made at home. Simply pour boiling water over the thick jelly-like threads and drink the smooth, mucilaginous water after it has brewed for a few minutes.

Corn silk tea can be highly beneficial as a kitchen remedy to relieve the pain of urinary-tract infections, such as cystitis, and for a gentle soothing of the entire urinary tract.

Corn silk might be difficult to obtain dried, as a prepared herb tea, but it is worth asking for. If you can't buy it, take pleasure in making your own home brew whenever sweet corn is in season.

COUCH-GRASS

(Agropyrum repens)

This common European and North African grass is not the blue couch or lawn couch commonly grown domestically. Although some of its properties are similar, a major difference is to be found in the plant's rhizome—the ground-running, root-producing stem.

The rhizome is the part used for herb tea preparation. It is a white, thick, clear root which grows just beneath the surface, where the grass runners spread and send down their hair roots at each junction. Have you ever watched a sick dog eat couch-grass? It is sensing, in its instinctive animal way, that couch-grass has a powerful diuretic effect to wash out infection from the kidneys and bladder.

Brewed from the dried, chopped-up roots, couchgrass herb tea is a powerful one and should be used only when some obvious pathology or trauma to the kidneys and bladder is in process.

Another problem that plagues many people is the weakness of the sphincter muscle of the bladder. When this condition prevails it is potentially socially dangerous for the sufferer to cough or sneeze. Elderly people particularly can use couchgrass tea to tighten and tone up the bladder sphincter and urinary tract to help overcome this distressing problem. The use of couch-grass tea in this way is verging on the medicinal, and it should be taken under professional direction rather than used as a general household tea.

DANDELION

(Taraxacum officinale)

If ever a plant was useful in "civilized" living, dandelion shares this distinction with chamomile. Its habit and place of growth will tell you that it is nudging humankind to make use of it. Dandelions grow around telegraph poles, on railway embankments, on pathways, under gravel and concrete, on rubbish dumps and roadsides, shouting their message of usefulness to that organ most overloaded by civilization, the human liver.

Although dandelion is frequently regarded as a herbal coffee substitute, it is brewed in the same way as herb tea and can be had as often as China tea or coffee.

The part of the plant most commonly used is the dried root, after it has been finely ground. Sometimes the leaves of the plant are added, or used separately for a milder brew.

Dandelion tea or coffee should be used as an everyday beverage in every household. Its use should not be restricted to occasional therapeutic doses and its contents will show you why. Dandelion contains many substances needed for a healthy human liver and it supports the function of the liver in its diversity of physiological roles.

Think of the liver as a chemical factory which converts food substances into fuel to make them available for the body to use. You can then better understand why dandelion is such a valuable plant—it helps to improve the functioning of the liver and its control over all those food additives, sprays, insecticides, pollutants and other chemical contaminants used by the precooked, frozen, prepackaged and processed food industry.

It is often difficult to live only on pure water and homegrown fresh foods and develop faith to avoid the perils of civilized living. But dandelion tea/coffee could be a factor to enable you to live with better health and better food absorption with less residual effect from contaminants.

Dandelion contains a balance of iron and calcium and several support substances, such as choline, to help you cope with cholesterol distri-

bution. It also contains vitamins A and D-2
(calciferol)—the vegetable variety of vitamin D.
Dandelion contains an average of about 15 percent starch, which varies seasonally, depending
on whether the plant is picked in spring or summer. The leaves, which have a very bitter taste,
stimulate the function of the gall bladder, as
well as the liver, in the production of bile and its
distribution into the intestinal tract. Dandelion
tea/coffee is especially helpful during that most
debilitating of illnesses, hepatitis, to support the
functions of the liver while the virus is still alive.

Vitamin B is also found in dandelion, an unusual vitamin to be found in the green part of
the plant because it is more usually found in
seeds. Supporting vitamin B, we find magnesium
salts for nerve function; sodium salts to give bodily suppleness and flexibility and to aid the circulation of fluids around the body; and silica, which
is helpful in driving out pockets of infection and
rubbish through the kidneys, the bowel and the
skin.

Most of the bitter taste of dandelion comes
from the mineral sulphur, essential in protein
and enzyme activity. It is also high in potassium,
vital to proper kidney function and muscle tone.
You can see that this cheery and irrepressible
plant is a complete package for the human liver.

I often prescribe dandelion tea/coffee as a regular
beverage for teenagers who are having difficulty
with acne and skin problems due to hormonal
change. I also prescribe it for people with metabolic difficulty with certain foods, for food allergy

sufferers, and for young children with allergic reactions to particular foods.

Dandelion tea/coffee is a healthful habit for modern living.

DILL SEED

(Anethum graveolens)

This is another plant of the family in which caraway, parsley, fennel, carrots, celery and aniseed are found. Dill aids and comforts the digestive tract. The seeds of the plant are the parts used to make tea and, as with any seeds, it is better to crush them slightly before pouring on the water, just off the boil, to make the tea.

Dill is another exception to the general rule that herb tea should be drunk while hot. It can be left to cool and put into a screwtop container in the refrigerator, then doled out in spoonfuls for dyspepsia. If you have difficulties with cucumber, sauerkraut, cabbage, coleslaw or raw onions; if you have difficulty eating seafood, especially shellfish; even if you have difficulty digesting capsicum; dill water can be used as a mild medicinal mixture after the meal.

The old-fashioned name for the tea made from dill is dill water. Indeed, it is still mentioned in many books on natural child-rearing as the best way to treat colic. A small teaspoon of dill water, after each feed, can help your baby to become contented and non-windy rather quickly.

Dill seeds, like all members of this botanical family, contain anethol, a substance which produces a quietening and calming effect on the gastro-intestinal tract. Many people would enjoy eating those raw foods mentioned above, if only they didn't suffer afterwards. The use of dill tea after such a meal could well be their answer.

ELDER FLOWERS

(Sambucus nigra)

Every book written about herbs and their use contains reference to various parts of the elder tree: the bark, berries, leaves and flowers. The first three should be prescribed only by qualified herbalists because their action in the body can be powerful. But the flowers of the elder are gentle indeed and can be used to brew a herb tea which is calming, soothing, broadly tonic and simultaneously relaxing.

If we look at the contents of the flowers, some idea of their usefulness as an everyday beverage can be obtained. Its mucilage is the basis of the plant's soothing effect on the gastric and alimentary canal. It contains two glycosides, sambunigrin and amygdalin (vitamin B-17), the latter also being found in apricot and almond kernels. These two glycosides are responsible for the tonic and energizing effect of elder flower tea. There is also choline for liver function, and a resin which takes the volatile oil of the plant with it and adheres to the digestive and alimentary tract all the way down, enabling good absorption of the herb's other properties to be made.

The flowers contain malic acid (also found in apples and stone fruits), which works within the bowel area to keep the pH (acid/alkaline) level at its optimum best for digestion. Acetic acid is also found in the flowers, helping to combat viral and influenza-type infections. Mineral compounds present in the flowers are potassium chloride for endocrine balance; potassium sulphate to help raise the body's immunity; sodium sulphate for fluid balance; magnesium phosphate and calcium phosphate for releasing tension and spasm in muscles and organs, and potassium nitrate, a mild heart stimulant.

It can be seen that elder flowers' effect as a herb tea is a broad general one for any of those conditions where you feel depressed and miserable. It is used as a common beverage throughout Europe and in parts of the United States, and I feel it could join the ranks of several other herb teas as an everyday beverage elsewhere in the world.

Externally, the tea can be used as a mild astringent and toning lotion for the skin. Dab elder flower tea on face and hands, around the neck, and on rough patches at elbows, knees and feet. Used regularly, such a lotion can help remove the odd wrinkle and improve skin tone and function. It can even be used as a comforting lotion for sunburn and mild skin infections. Use the remains of your elder flower tea as a splash-on toner after a shower and even use the cool tea as a lotion for your eyes. Although it is certainly not specific enough to improve vision or to correct serious eye conditions, it is soothing and comforting to apply to sore eyes after a day's driving, after city smog or summertime glare on the beach.

Use elder flowers in all these ways to save money on cosmetics and to support you through some of the earlier stages of infective illnesses with a maximum of comfort.

EQUISETUM

(Equisetum arvense)

Equisetum is a strange little plant, resembling grey-green asparagus and growing in a manner to suggest that it likes to keep close to the earth to acquire most avidly the minerals from the soil in which it grows. It is often regarded as a common weed, being found throughout much of North America, Europe and Asia. Some people know it better by its common name of "shave grass".

The bunched-up stems of equisetum have gentle abrasive qualities and were once used to polish pewter, silver and other soft metals. Luckily, this abrasive quality is not repeated quite so strongly in the human intestinal tract!

Of all commonly used therapeutic herbs, equisetum provides the highest source of silica. The plant contains, as well as the enormous number of silicate compounds, salts of calcium and magnesium, which ensure that this silica is correctly absorbed.

It is certainly not a tea to be drunk in large quantities every day. Neither is equisetum a quiet and gentle tea to make you feel good. Its action in the body is anything but quiet because it tends to powerfully stimulate kidneys and bowel and sets about chemically changing any concretions found in the body, such as stone, gravel and even such thickened tissue as adhesions and fibroids.

If in doubt about drinking equisetum tea, it is best to check with a herbal practitioner. For some people its powerful stimulative and elimative action can be very uncomfortable indeed. As a compensation for its noise and fire, it helps to grow strong fingernails, luxuriant hair and good tooth enamel. But for many people equisetum tea can be just too disturbing.

I prescribe equisetum tea for some arthritics and some patients with fluid retention, but discomfort can be felt in areas of the body where arthritic nodes and spurs can be stirred mightily by the silica "arrows." If your naturopath recommends equisetum tea for you, follow the instructions accurately and you should not suffer any of the more stringent effects which this herb can produce.

EUCALYPTUS

(Eucalyptus globulus)

It's an amazing statement for an Australian herbalist to have to make, but it is a fact that the
eucalyptus tree is hardly used as a dried herb in
its native country.

Have you ever picked leaves from a gum tree
on a picnic and dropped two in your ordinary tea
to add to the flavor? Add the fresh or dried leaves
of the eucalyptus, in all its many varieties, to
any other beverage and you do two things—
improve flavor and provide a valuable therapeutic agent. The aromatic, penetrating and antiseptic
fragrance of the eucalyptus is known the world
over for clearing the head and the respiratory
passages of the upper sinus and the bronchial
tree. A few leaves from a eucalyptus tree will
provide just a touch of the eucalyptus oil they
contain, without being too strong and without
spoiling the flavor of whatever other beverage
they are added to.

Eucalyptus oil, extracted from the leaves of
many varieties, is well known to herbalists all
around the world, being used specifically for bronchial complaints and coughs. But in Australia,
where the plant grows so prolifically, it is rarely
used or sought—a case of familiarity breeding
contempt?

Eucalyptus gives a lift and an extra zing of

flavor when added to other beverages. Herbal product manufacturers should add a few dried eucalyptus leaves to many of their cough and bronchial teas for the double benefits offered.

EYEBRIGHT

(Euphrasia officinalis)

There are many herbalists who use and recommend eyebright internally to improve the eyesight. But in my experience, it can be much better employed when brewed as a tea for bathing the eyes externally.

Eyebright is a small annual herb which enjoys temperate climates and contains strong resins. These are internally upsetting to many people, creating a disturbing effect on the liver, even to producing nausea and dizziness. As a therapeutic aid, eyebright tea is far more valuable as an externally applied agent than as a beverage. An application of the tea-strength solution once a day should be sufficient to soothe burning, irritated eyelids assaulted by smog, cigarette smoke, car exhaust fumes or chemical sprays. It can also relieve tired eyes resulting from intensive reading or studying.

FLAX SEED

(Linum usitatissimum)

Linseed

The flax plant is related to the nettle family. Like nettles, flax stems contain fibers which can be treated and woven into fine-quality linen. For this reason it has been a useful plant for centuries.

Flax is an annual herb, with small blue flowers and a hard brown, shiny, oily envelope around the soft-centered seeds, often called "linseeds." Some 15 percent of the weight of these seeds is a soft lubricating mucilage, soothing to an irritated or inflamed digestive tract. A tea can be made from the whole seeds, which should be crushed a little in a mortar and pestle (or with the kitchen mallet, having first put the seeds in a plastic bag). This tea can be quite useful as a mild laxative tea, particularly when a *dry* bowel is the cause of constipation.

Flax seed tea can be taken by quite young babies and by elderly people because it does not cause griping or strong movements of the bowel. It can be effectively given after surgery on the bowel, or after any surgery where bowel functions might be impaired. It is also beneficial if drugs have induced iatrogenic constipation, by aiding the bowel to recommence its natural functioning.

The inner part of flax seeds comprise 30 to 40

percent of fixed oil and about 25 percent protein compound, including albumin, plus waxes, resins and sugars. The seeds are high in phosphorus compounds and contain lecithin in their soft pulpy center. Lecithin is also a phosphorus compound, and plays a major role in maintaining cholesterol balance in the body and in overcoming nervous debilitation.

Flax seed tea is also useful for urinary tract infections and for inflammation in the kidney or bladder caused by stones or gravel.

Linseed, as most people call flax seed, is often used as a porridge meal. It is favored because it is a natural high source of vegetable proteins and valuable polyunsaturated fats, but such a meal may be too heavy for some people to digest. The tea form is an excellent therapeutic aid because flax seed can gradually help normalize bowel function without danger and without pain.

FENNEL

(Foeniculum vulgare)

Fennel is often mentioned with respect and just as often with a great deal of misinformation. Fennel seems to have two major stories told about it—the first relating to its effect on eyesight and the second relating to its "slimming" uses. This delightfully intriguing information about fennel can be inaccurately based and the effect of the plant in the body should be well understood before its use.

The fennel plant is regarded as a common weed in most parts of the world, growing, like the dandelion, round the edges of civilization. It seems to shout at us that it is useful in such conditions as polluted atmospheres, as a therapeutic aid when the diet contains anything but "simple" food, and when water supplies are less than "pure." Its tall umbrella-shaped yellow flowers, with the feathery leaves underneath, can be seen clambering up wire fences and stone walls, or growing in the most inhospitable, dank and polluted conditions.

A favorite place for fennel is on roadsides, where the exhaust fumes from passing motor traffic do not seem to deter it at all. Certainly, there is enough fennel available for everyone to pick the ripe brown seeds in late summer and store them for use throughout the year.

If you live in areas where fennel hasn't started to grow, the dried seeds are readily available as a packaged tea. The aniseed flavor of fennel is cooling and pleasing to the palate and its pleasant taste as a herb tea should make it more often used. It can be added to blends, with caraway or parsley, or it can be used on its own to get the cooling effect of the anethol—the oil found in all this Umbelliferae class of plant.

Among its many usages, fennel tea has been employed as an eye lotion since the earliest days of herbal recording. It is a mild and pleasant lotion to dab on and around the eyes, similar to the way elder flower water can be used. Its most effective result is on the yellow patches in the white of the eye, known as pterygium. If the whites of your eyes are a dirty yellow or, even worse, if the dirty yellow is streaked with inflamed blood vessels, fennel tea dabbed on the eyes can give comfort and a clearer and brighter color. Those yellowy patches are indicative of your body's difficulty in absorbing fats. Dabbing fennel tea on eyes that look like poached eggs is symptomatic treatment only and certainly not a miracle cure.

The "slimming" reputation of fennel involves its action in stimulating, normalizing and balancing the pancreas. The biochemistry of pancreas function is complex. Simply stated, the pancreas plays a major role, together with the liver and the gall bladder, in metabolism, especially of fats and sugars.

If your liver is laboring under a load of inferior quality food, if your diet is full of "take-away" and "instant packaged" processed foods, fennel tea could certainly help you to lose a little weight—*if* the weight is directly attributable to difficult assimilation of fats and sugars. For those people whose weight is due to fluid retention or endocrine imbalance, or any other of a thousand different causes, fennel tea, sadly, might not have any reducing effect.

The tea can be drunk by diabetic patients, not as a treatment but as a support for a pancreas laboring with sugar difficulties. Fennel tea has a slightly laxative effect for some people and it increases the appetite of others for better foods. No longer do they want the refined or greasy carbohydrates and filling fats, but find it much easier to balance their diets with raw fruits and vegetables and other natural foods.

The nutritional and therapeutic properties of fennel are indeed complex. High in mineral salts—mostly compounds of sodium, potassium and sulphur—plus about 50 to 60 percent of that volatile oil anethol (which helps to settle queazy stomachs), fennel provides the elements necessary for efficient digestion of fats. Fennel seeds also contain sugar and starch in a balanced form which should neither raise nor lower sugar levels in diabetics.

FENUGREEK

(Trigonella foenumgraecum)

The fenugreek plant is an annual, growing about 2 feet high. It is a native of Greece and other Mediterranean countries, spreading as far afield as the Middle East and Asia. The tea is made from the seeds of the plant and your first cup of fenugreek tea should tell you that it is more like a broth than a sweet dessert-type tea.

In the culinary arts, fenugreek is one of the spices used to make curry, so you can imagine that its pungent taste does not blend well with

A SAMPLER OF HERBS FOR TEA

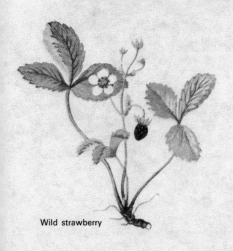

Wild strawberry

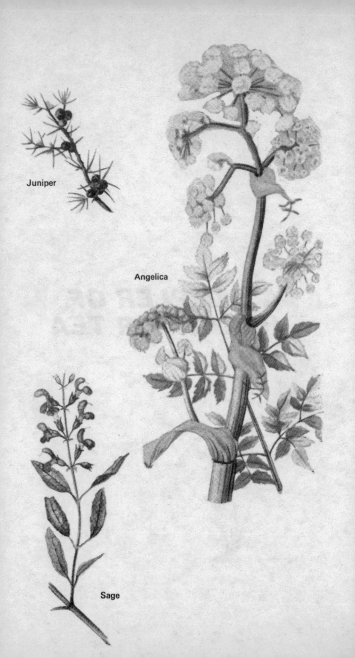

Juniper

Angelica

Sage

Wild celery

Great burdock

Coltsfoot

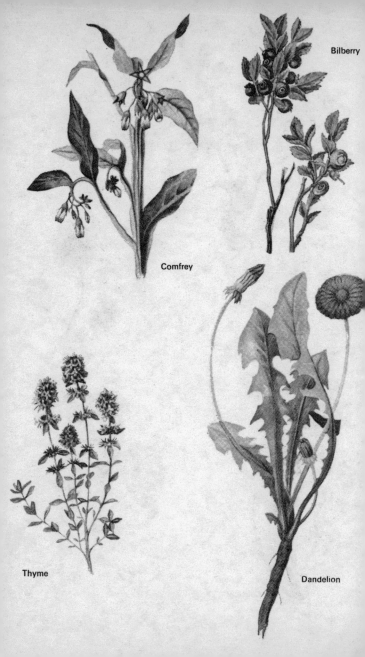

Bilberry

Comfrey

Thyme

Dandelion

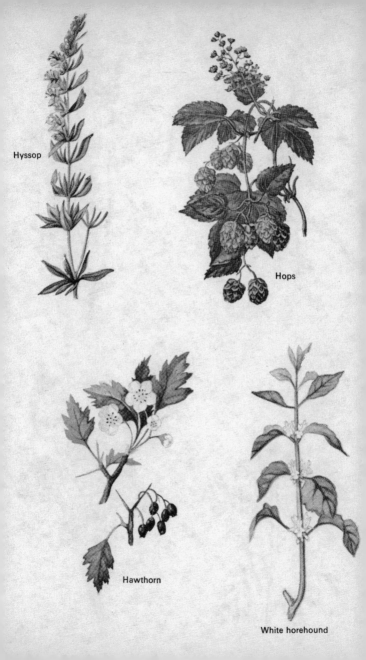

Hyssop

Hops

Hawthorn

White horehound

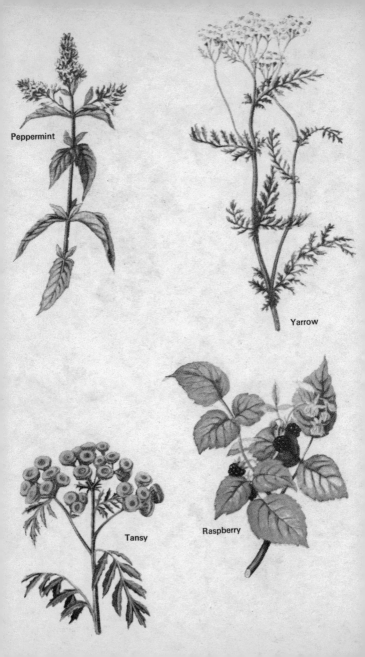

Peppermint

Yarrow

Tansy

Raspberry

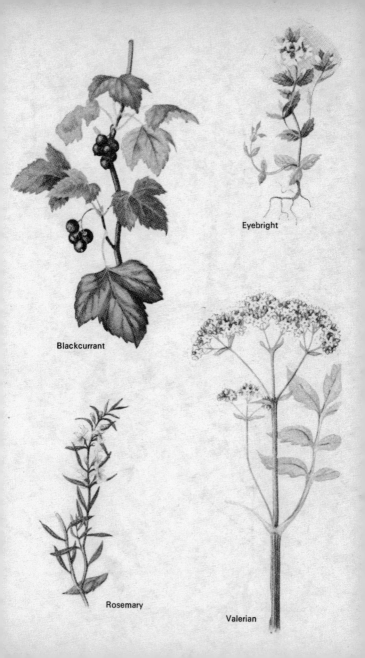

Eyebright

Blackcurrant

Rosemary

Valerian

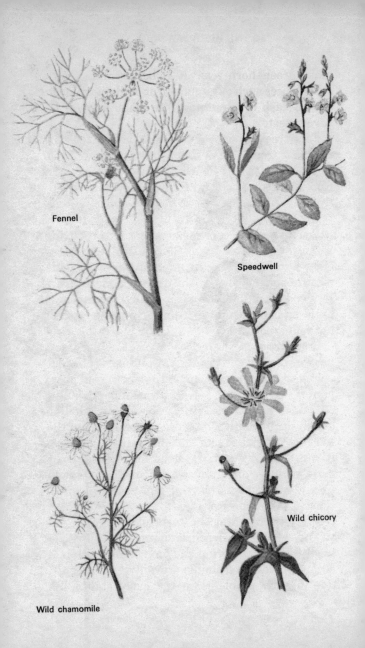

Fennel

Speedwell

Wild chicory

Wild chamomile

other green herb teas. It is better mixed with other spices such as cinnamon or cardamom, even with a dash of horseradish, to make more of its savory taste.

Fenugreek is one of the most useful teas for the home treatment of simple infective conditions. Those miseries experienced in head colds—catarrh from blocked ears, aching sinuses—can be speedily relieved by one or two cups of hot fenugreek tea.

Fenugreek is one of the best teas for producing perspiration. It is equally useful in reducing a fever and its unclogging effect in the body is its most important virtue. Mucus can be more easily coughed up and blown out and further catarrhal build-up can be minimized after a cup or two of hot fenugreek tea.

Like fennel, fenugreek is a useful tea for those people who have difficulty with fat absorption. It is rich in mineral salts, particularly in iron phosphate, which has a powerful burning-out effect on minor infections. The seeds contain choline and lecithin, both substances necessary for the liver to metabolize fats and oils. Infused as a tea, it can often prevent the need for antibiotics or more intrusive and intensive drug therapy if taken in the early stages of viral and bacterial infections of the respiratory tract.

Many people find the taste of fenugreek tea strange. Persevere with fenugreek if your body tends towards catarrhal and bronchial complaints because it can be a simple preventive and corrective of such problems in the early stages. Its flavor may become more acceptable as you gain relief by drinking it.

Help your teenage son or daughter remove some of the miseries of acne with an occasional cup of fenugreek tea. Its effect on the skin is slower and less obvious, but its high vitamin A and D-2 content helps to normalize skin function which can suffer badly from hormonal disturbance at puberty. B vitamins are also found in the seeds (as they are in all seeds), as well as a glycoside called Trigonellin, a good energy producer in the body.

GINGER

(Zingiber officinale)

One does not think often of ginger as a base for making herbal tea. As a powdered spice it is often added to herbal tea blends to give them the "zing" from Zingiber! Its piquant taste helps to liven many flatter and broader tastes in the plant world, but its use as an ingredient in herb tea is specifically to help those folks with under-active stomachs, who have difficulty in manufacturing or secreting adequate hydrochloric acid to digest their food. Any herb tea blend containing a touch of ginger can improve the appetite of such people by stimulating saliva secretion in the mouth which can, in turn, stimulate gastric acid production. The Chinese understand the digestive properties of ginger and often add it to their foods.

Ginger is a perennial plant, indigenous to most tropical regions of eastern Asia. It is now extensively cultivated throughout most tropical and sub-tropical countries, especially China and India. The rootstock is that part of the plant from which the well known ginger flavor derives, and it keeps almost indefinitely when dried.

Choose a herb tea blend containing ginger for those children who gulp their food too quickly or those adults who eat and run. It is also highly beneficial for people who gulp down a hasty carbohydrate breakfast and regret it all the way through the morning. Any herb tea containing ginger can help to remove wind accumulated in the digestive tract and reduce the social dangers of flatulence after a rapidly consumed meal.

GINSENG

(Panax schin-seng)

Asian Ginseng

(Panax quinque folium)

American Ginseng

This plant has been so commercially promoted that many of its properties and the claims made about them seem to appear so magical that one would imagine ginseng to be an absolute necessity, even to enable one to get up in the morning. As with any commercially-promoted product, one must delve a little deeper into the facts to establish when ginseng tea is a benefit and when it is absolutely unnecessary.

Formerly obtainable as a wild perennial, the ginseng plant is now so sought-after that it is commercially cultivated. It is a plant with a uniquely-shaped root, from which its highly-prized properties derive. The Manchurian and Korean species are the most sought-after, although the cheaper American variety is increasingly used as a substitute.

Ginseng tea is brewed from the finely ground dried root. Its primary effect on the body is on one target area, the pituitary gland. Every other effect experienced when taking ginseng is a direct result of improved function of this gland. The pituitary, with its conductor-of-the-orchestra control of the body, can set the pace, tone and volume of almost every other bodily process.

You can now see why so many claims are made for ginseng. But care should be taken when using it. For instance, ginseng tea should not be used by children whose pace is already pretty hectic. It is not specifically indicated for adults who are naturally speedy or hyperactive. If you are painfully thin, and your every action is performed with lightning speed, ginseng tea can have a decidedly disturbing effect.

The value of ginseng is to be felt primarily by those thicker and more solid folk who need a bit of a prod, a bit of a lift, a bit of an increase in volume and speed in their daily doings. Ginseng

[58]

is most likely to have the best general effect for these people if taken in the form of tea.

I feel strongly that ginseng and its effect on Western bodies is not yet completely understood. While the tea strength of the product is not sufficient to disturb body functions in the short term, I would certainly recommend its use only over short periods of time to provide the best tonic effect. In the long term, its more subtle influences are, as yet, not sufficiently understood.

One of the major chemical compounds in ginseng is an iodine salt. This is combined with phosphorus compounds to stimulate pituitary and thyroid function. The result of an excess of these chemicals in the body can be supercharged activity for hyperactive people. Ginseng tea is quite unnecessary for those who buzz with a constant charge of adrenal energy.

For those slower, more lethargic people, ginseng can provide a desirable and occasional stimulant after a period of heavy physical work or mental exhaustion. It is best used to get a quick, short-term, tonic effect to return you to normal functional speed.

GOLDEN SEAL ROOT

(Hydrastis canadensis)

What a boon the North American Indian pharmacopoeia has given to us with this plant. The yellow stain from the root was used for centuries as face paint and eventually some observant European colonizers noticed that skin and eye diseases disappeared when this long-lasting dye was used ceremonially. It was then only a step to employing it therapeutically in ointments and tinctures for relieving such conditions.

As an herb tea, golden seal root has what could best be described as an internally detergent effect. It loosens away from the mucous linings any "dirt"—bacteria, irritant particles, acid remnants and unexpelled rubbish which are so often found in the bowel. This cleansing is simultaneously highly antiseptic.

As with most plant roots possessing a pronounced yellow stain, golden seal root is rich in vitamin A and resin. But it also contains an alkaloid, hydrastine, which indicates this tea should not be taken in excess.

The best way to use golden seal root tea is as a "spring clean" for the inner body. Drink a cup each day or each second day, depending on the level of your bodily toxicity. Maintain this for a ten-day period, then discontinue. Every machine needs a hosing off or a steam clean at times—the human body, while not exactly a machine, responds well to regular cleansing. Golden seal root tea can be effectively used in this way, occasionally, as an herbal insurance against "rust, coking up or dirty filters."

HAWTHORN

(Crataegus oxyacantha)

The dried berries of the small hawthorn tree, a native of Europe and Northern Asia, have been used for centuries in home herbal treatment of circulatory disorders. It is one of those teas better used for a specific purpose, supporting the function of the major circulation. As such, it can be taken as a general beverage, with safety, by patients with cardiac problems.

Hawthorn tea is brewed from the dried berries and sometimes the flowers of the plant. It can have an energizing effect on elderly people and is similar to maté tea in that it can be drunk occasionally when one is tired after periods of hard physical work.

By assisting to regulate heart action, hawthorn tea can normalize blood pressure and it can be regarded as an antispasmodic. It tones the major blood vessels and can be especially recommended for anyone under major circulatory stress.

HIBISCUS

(Malva sylvestris)

The rich ruby color of hibiscus tea (sometimes called malva tea) is a tonic to the eyes and the stomach. One of the very richest flower sources of iron, copper and vitamin C, the tea is often blended with rosehips to give added color and extra flavor. Hibiscus tea is also regarded as a mild antispasmodic and a nerve nourisher.

Hibiscus flowers are dried and desiccated to provide one of the more recently discovered herb teas. Its refreshing and astringent taste is as easy on the palate as its bright color is on the eyes. It is readily available in dried form, and tea bags are available for convenience.

With modern packaging and processing of herbal products to ensure that they are dried effectively with all the ingredients intact, it is possible to explore a much wider range of flavors and tastes than one can grow in the backyard or pick from the roadside. This enables the exotic flavors and colors of far-off lands to be introduced as new and delightful herb tea experiences. Occasionally, new herb tea blends come onto the market with hibiscus as an attractive and nourishing ingredient. One especially delicious and refreshing blend combines hibiscus with rosehips and peppermint to brighten one's day.

HOPS

(Humulus lupulus)

Everyone knows about hops in beer. Fewer people are aware that the same relaxant and calming effects of hops can be gained by drinking tea made from the flowers.

Beer brewed at home the old way, where fermentation was not stopped artificially and the beer was matured naturally on the yeast, was a form of herbal beverage which had strong recommendations as a medicinal drink. But few people realize that it is possible to get the calming effect of one or two beers after work by having one or two cups of hops tea instead, without any of the alcoholic disturbance that goes with beer.

Long used as a herbal tea for sleeplessness, dried hops can also be used to make hops pillows, small sachets which can be placed under your pillow at night. The refreshing odor of the oil from the hops can soothe your body's sleep reflexes all night. Hops tea, drunk the last thing before retiring, can do the same thing.

Hops contain phosphates of calcium, magnesium and potassium. All these compounds act towards releasing and relaxing body tensions. Two substances, humulone and lupulone, are bitter ingredients found in hops flowers and offering special properties for toning the physical nervous system. A cup of hops tea, or a blended sleeping tea which contains hops flowers as one of its ingredients, can be a highly preferred alternative to some sedatives.

HOREHOUND

(Marrubium vulgare)

This plant is a common pasture weed in Australia, North America and Europe. It is found in uncultivated wasteland and grazing land. There are two varieties, white and black. Both can be readily used as herb teas, although this drink is *not* a pleasant introduction to herb tea drinking. It is extremely bitter and sufficiently astringent to make it difficult for some people to swallow. However, it has an age-old reputation as a country remedy for coughs and colds in the head and chest. The fact that it is freely available in pastures recommends it to many rural people.

In its dried form, horehound is often blended with fenugreek, licorice and thyme as a bronchial tea to help loosen heavy mucus. Horehound tea does not cure a cold, but it does speed up the eliminatory process and powerfully tones the mucous linings of the respiratory system.

To be more orally acceptable, horehound is better blended with less bitter herbs. Its bitter resin, marrubin, its content of fat and wax, and the resinous oils which adhere to the respiratory mucous linings make it a most powerful agent for moving and loosening hard or congealed mucus.

HUCKLEBERRY

(Vaccinium pennsylvanicum)

Purely an American plant, the huckleberry is rarely used in other parts of the world. Drink the tea as you would blueberry or black currant— they are all tangy fruit teas. Mix and match huckleberry with lemon and/or spice teas for a variety of delightful flavors. In the winter, the addition of a cinnamon stick to your hot brew will provide a very warming beverage—in summer, added mint will provide cooling refreshment.

As with all teas brewed from berry fruits, vitamin C and rutin are valuable nutrients found in attendance. However, the quantities are not sufficient for these teas to be regarded as sources of therapeutic dosages of either nutrient. But for day to day needs, the quantities present will be found beneficial.

JASMINE

(Jasminium officinale)

For many centuries the Orientals have highly regarded jasmine tea as a special beverage with two seemingly contrary effects. Some consider the drink to offer mildly tranquilizing properties to the nerves, others regard it as having special

aphrodisiac properties. The dried petals of the
jasmine flowers and the leaves (from which the
tea is brewed) possess traces of alkalizing compounds which could exert a mild sedating affect on
the body's nervous system. For this reason the
herb tea is traditionally regarded as an excellent
pre-meal beverage. In Western society, it may
prevent nervous indigestion.

Its sweet flower-taste makes it a pleasant tea
to offer guests *after* a meal, too, instead of the
usual coffee.

JUNIPER

(Juniperus communis)

The bluish-tinted berries of the juniper tree have
been used for centuries, mixed with other ingredients, to make gin. Used as a herb tea, the
berries have a powerful stimulatory effect on kidney function, urine secretion and fluid retention.
Many people with chronic edema (fluid retention)
can drink juniper tea regularly, but not heavily,
as a mild corrective for kidneys slow to secrete
urine, which causes fluid to be retained in the
body tissues.

As an evergreen shrub, juniper is widely indigenous throughout most of the Americas, Europe and Asia. It flowers each spring, but the
berries require two years to ripen to a dark purple, when they are ready for picking and drying.

Juniper berry tea is not to be drunk by the bucketful! In fact, it is a tea to have only during periods of fluid retention—say, one cup a day, sipped slowly. As soon as the edematous swelling reduces, the ankles return to normal size and the wrists lose their lumpiness, it is better to discontinue this tea.

One of its best home uses is as an immediate treatment for cystitis. Many cystitis infections originate in the kidneys rather than in the bladder. A cup of juniper tea taken every two to three hours during a painful attack of cystitis can flush out the kidneys and the entire urinary tract to remove irritants and reduce infection. This flushing action of the herb is its most specific attribute. Logically then, its use should not be taken to such an extreme that the kidneys are overworked.

Juniper is a significant source of potassium and oily resins which adhere to kidney tissues, taking this potassium with them. There is also a balance of sodium salts to assist the potassium to "pump" into the kidneys. Because the potassium content is in higher proportion than is normally found in the sodium/potassium ratio, it is not wise to prolong juniper berry tea drinking past the point where fluid retention has gone and body tissues are back to normal.

A little barley water can be beneficially added to juniper berry tea for relief from cystitis. This mixture can be a boon to people suffering acute symptoms, but if the condition does not clear they would be wise to see a professional practitioner for advice. If, in spite of juniper tea drinking, fluid retention is still obvious, further advice should always be sought.

Juniper berries can be beneficially added to general diuretic mixtures of herbs. Juniper can be found in most blended teas which are specifically prepared for kidney and urinary function. In these blends, the amount of juniper berries is usually balanced so that there is not such a positive and powerful stimulus to kidneys as when taken alone.

LEMON

(Citrus limonia)

The common lemon is one of the best additives to any herb tea. A slice of lemon naturally perks up the flavor of a drink, but the oil in lemon rind adds a special dimension to any herb tea—an antiseptic quality. Lemon is often added to many herb tea blends for a flavor boost, especially in milder herb teas.

Lemon contains vitamins C, P and K and the mineral calcium. This offers an excellent combination to stimulate the commencement of healing processes, and to assist in their continuation. These nutrients also support the blood quality, as well as aiding damaged tissue repair.

LEMON BALM

(Melissa officinalis)

Often called melissa, lemon balm is a native of eastern Mediterranean countries and western Asia. This herb was originally used in the Arab world to make a tea which could produce a mild perspiration. Under the thick, yet light, clothing worn by the inhabitants of these countries, lemon balm tea produced a marked cooling effect as perspiration was promoted and then recondensed to provide a water-jacket insulation effect.

Lemon balm is sometimes called "the scholar's herb," although it is absolutely no use drinking a cup of this tea just prior to a final examination! One needs to drink it frequently while studying to help clear the head and freshen the senses. It is reputed to exercise a beneficial effect on the memory and this could certainly help in preparation for an examination.

The taste of lemon balm tea is similar to that of a sweet mint tea with a touch of added lemon. When used in combination with other sweet-flavored herb teas, it can be a pleasant taste sensation for children of all ages.

The action of lemon balm lies in its balance of the minerals sodium and chlorine. These combine effectively to prevent excessive metabolite loss during the process of perspiration. As a mild digestive aid, lemon balm tea is especially beneficial in hot weather, as well as being useful as a refreshing, cooling drink to revive a "hot" head and body.

LICORICE

(Glycyrrhiza glabra)

Deriving from a perennial plant growing wild in the lower parts of Europe and Asia, the sweet taste of licorice has become the confectionary favorite of many generations. The root and woodstock of the licorice plant provide the source of the blackened delight on the faces, tongues and fingers of virtually all children at some time in their lives.

Licorice is a valuable source of iron salts and is one of nature's gentlest and yet most effective laxatives. When brewed into a tea, licorice retains its important therapeutic properties and also provides a very tasteful beverage which is surprisingly sweet and "more-ish." In fact, it leaves such a pleasant after-taste that many people find it a most refreshing drink and very soothing for the throat.

But the most valuable property of licorice tea is its laxative power. Too many people, especially children, develop the habit of *not* developing the habit of regular bowel evacuations. Excuses such as "it's inconvenient to take the time," or "I'll miss something," or "the toilet is not clean in public places when I'm away from home," or a thousand and one other problems which often give rise to constipation. Such "holding off" creates a dry bowel whose walls have removed so much residual liquid from the feces (due to their unduly long stay) that when the bowels finally do move, straining and discomfort, even hemorrhoids and bleeding, can result. Licorice has a softening effect on hard, compacted fecal matter. Such a simple and pleasant therapeutic aid surprises most people, but nature teaches us so often that her simple abundance is there to be used.

LINDEN

*(Tilia americana and
tilia europaea)*

Both the European and American lime trees are deciduous, often growing to well over one hundred feet in height. Often known as linden trees, they both produce leaves and flowers which have long been employed for their herbal properties; those of the American variety generally have the stronger sedative, anti-depressant effect, while the European leaves and flowers are milder, more like chamomile in action.

This herb tea has a gentle flavor, is lightly perfumed and makes an excellent late-afternoon social drink over which the affairs of the day can be discussed in a happy, relaxed atmosphere. This prepares one for the enjoyment of a nourishing evening meal which of course is so much more beneficial when the body is relaxed and its food intake can be most efficiently assimilated, free from any tension or turmoil.

This tea is especially pleasant in summer, for it offers a delightful cooling effect on the throat and body. Some people prefer to drink it cold in summer, hot in winter. Whichever way it is consumed, linden tea is a most desirable pre-dinner drink. It can help the cares of the day slide away as easily as the pleasant fluid slides down the throat.

MATÉ

(Ilex paraguariensis)

I remember my grandmother brewing her daily pot of strong green maté tea, her white hair shining and her blue eyes twinkling with fun. She ascribed much of her energy and good health (at eighty-four years of age) to drinking this strong concoction every day. And never a day went by when my grandmother was not working hard!

Maté tea has long been regarded as a safe, general stimulant during periods of hard, physical work. However, it does contain small amounts of caffeine and oxalic acid, so care should be exercised in the frequency of its use. It is best taken on its own because the flavor does not blend easily.

The maté bush is a native of the temperate central area of South America—its botanical name taken from the country in which it is most abundant, Paraguay. It is a member of the holly family, producing the characteristic small, reddish holly berries and tiny white flowers. But it is the leaves and, occasionally, the stems from which the characteristic maté tea is made—the drink which has become known as the equivalent of coffee in terms of its stimulating properties. The strong, bitter/astringent brew is the regular drink of the tough, outdoor, high-country dwellers of Paraguay, northern Argentina and southern Brazil. You too will find that a cup of maté tea tones up the muscles, especially the smooth muscle of the heart.

Like many plants native to high altitudes, maté, when brewed into a tea, supports oxygen flow around the body. It also supplies salts of iron and potassium from which the muscles of the body derive added energy. Adding a pinch of vegetable salt or a slice of lemon to this tonic restorative tea will greatly improve the flavor for people who do not normally drink such strong brews.

NETTLE

(Urtica dioica)

Everyone knows the acid sting of the common nettle. But this plant has many valuable properties which far outweigh its discomforting reputation.

The dried, green leaves of this common perennial make a very useful herb tea for people with low blood pressure, anemia and other symptoms of lack of good arterial blood flow in the body. An "arterial tonic" is an appropriate way to describe nettle tea.

Another of our "civilized" plants, nettle grows almost everywhere. It is to be found around barnyards and home paddocks, along roadsides and against fences, in fact almost every block of wasteland will be seen to support some common nettle in nearly every country of the world. But nettle needs plenty of moisture and a soil containing adequate animal manure and/or organic matter to grow to its dark green, medicinal best.

The stinging hairs of the nettle are no longer a human hazard once the plant has been cut and dried in preparation for its brewing into herb tea or its equally valuable use as a herbal ointment. Fresh nettles can be used as a brew for herb tea, or perhaps lightly steamed as a green vegetable. Once hot water has been added, the sting of the nettle is inactivated, as the carbonic and formic acids are quickly broken down into harmless compounds.

Nettle contains iron and phosphorus and is an excellent source of both these minerals. However, care should be taken not to drink quantities of nettle tea if one tends towards hypertension. Nettle tea can increase blood pressure and is more suitable for tired people with poor circulation than for overwrought, tense worriers.

PAPAYA

(Carica papaya)

One of the most popular warm-climate fruits, known everywhere around the world, is the papaya. In some countries, it is called "paw paw," but wherever it is grown, it is consumed with avid enjoyment. Papaya is a tropical and subtropical fruit tree with huge, green leaves and yellow-golden fruit. It is easy to grow, easy to harvest and extremely nutrient-rich, both in fruit and leaves.

Although not regarded as one of the most popular herb teas, papaya leaf tea has many valuable properties for therapeutic employment. It is a strongly astringent tea with an anti-parasitic and vermicidal action. In being effective at killing off many varieties of intestinal worms, papaya leaf tea is especially beneficial to people living in tropical climates. It is as though nature intended us to employ her "local" products, for intestinal parasites are far more prevalent in tropical regions, which is where papaya trees abound.

Travellers in Asian, African and some Latin countries often find they must restrict their food intake to guard against parasitic invasion. In some countries, no matter how careful you are, intestinal upsets will occur, as most visitors to Mexico have discovered, for instance. Always take along some papaya leaf tea and drink a cup of it at least once a day when traveling through such regions. It is the best insurance you can have.

PARSLEY

(Petroselinum crispum or petroselinum sativum)

So many varieties of parsley are grown and occur naturally in almost every country of the world that it is impossible to consider each one individually. But therapeutically, only two varieties are strongly medicinal—the common curled and, even stronger, the Italian straight-leaf varieties.

There is so much of almost every nutrient and so many therapeutic properties in parsley that it is hard to give an order of preference for its virtues. Parsley leaf contains vitamins B, C and E, the alkalizing minerals calcium, iron and potassium, as well as the appetite and digestive stimulants, apiol and apiine. The potassium salts are responsible for making parsley leaf tea a powerful diuretic and a strong heart, kidney and liver tonic.

No matter how parsley is taken, whether as a vegetable, garnish or herb tea, it is sometimes the most nutritious part of the meal. Parsley is such a strong tonic to the body that it should not be drunk to excess; every day is too much. Body fluids are stimulated to move more rapidly and there is strong excitation of nerve plexuses right thru the body, improving the quality of the messages carried. Arthritis sufferers may find that parsley tea gives them more positive excretion of uric acid and stimulates kidney function generally. The improvement in the pain of the disease can be an added benefit as nerve reactions are strengthened.

Parsley leaf tea may be used as a "blood tonic." For any disease where blood quality is less than good, it can be drunk every few days until there is improvement. Of course, it is only a general support for such diseases which will certainly need therapeutic correction as well. Eating the fresh green sprigs of parsley with a meal lessens the need for parsley leaf tea.

PENNYROYAL

(Mentha pulegium)

Wrongly classed by many herb books as "an abortive," pennyroyal appears to have developed a reputation based on ignorance and supposition. It will most certainly not help to terminate a pregnancy, but if a period is missed due to a chill, a shock, emotional trauma, even fatiguing travel, pennyroyal tea can restore the usual menstrual flow by gently adjusting hormones back to normal.

A native of northern Europe, pennyroyal is a perennial which grows best in moist shade. It is a creeping plant, giving off a characteristic, pleasant aroma and producing clusters of smallish, purple flower stems in summer. The complete plant lends itself to drying for herb tea preparation, with a mint-like flavor and a pleasant coolness to the palate.

Pennyroyal tea should not be used on a regular basis. It offers specific benefits for occasional therapeutic use and should be drunk mainly for its corrective properties. A cup of pennyroyal tea taken each day of the week prior to the usual commencement of a period has helped many women who have suffered from pre-menstrual tension and cramps. For children, its mild anti-depressant properties can also be of benefit if taken only occasionally. Its pleasant flavor might tempt you to drink it more often, but always treat it as a purely medicinal beverage.

PEPPERMINT

(Mentha piperita)

The strongest in flavor of all the mint family, peppermint has a flavor most people know well and enjoy. The plant is easy to grow, likes sun and moisture, but dies back and disappears in the winter months.

Peppermint is a hybrid perennial plant originating in the cooler temperate regions of North America and Europe, although it is now found throughout the world as a cultivated herb. The leaves lend themselves perfectly to herb tea brewing, either fresh or dried. However, as the fresh leaves are not readily available in winter or spring, the dried form can always be found in health food stores.

As a hot beverage in winter, or as a cool drink or the base for a fruit punch in summer, peppermint is easily one of the most popular of all herb teas. It is sold in tea bags, loose, or as a basis of blended herb teas, and is also available in the modern form of an instant tea. But the risk with instantizing is that some of the valuable and characteristic menthol oil will be lost during the process.

As a settler for overloaded, windy stomachs, peppermint tea has no equal. After that business lunch, the birthday party or that enormous annual gorge—the Christmas dinner—sit back and sip a cup of freshly brewed peppermint tea. Its menthol oil is a valuable digestive enzyme stimulant, which also leaves the palate feeling freshened. Combined with alfalfa, its digestive benefits are accentuated—hence the deserved popularity of alfalfa-mint tea after a meal.

Hot peppermint tea can be a marvellous drink for anyone suffering from the clogged head that goes with a cold or influenza. Children, especially, respond to its powerful menthol cleansing action when they feel their breathing become easier and their upper sinuses, respiratory passages and throat begin to clear. The addition of a slice of lemon and/or a small spoon of honey will further increase the palatability of this already-pleasant herb tea.

RASPBERRY

(Rubus striqosus or
Rubus idaeus)

These slightly different varieties of raspberry bush offer leaves which brew into a very useful herb tea. The former variety is found primarily throughout North America and is distinguished by its prickly stems; the latter is indigenous to Europe and has few, if any, prickles. Both varieties grow wild in untended fields and forests, producing a red, summer-ripening fruit. The leaves of the wild raspberry produce the best tea.

For centuries raspberry leaf tea has been a well known and oft-used support for pregnant women. A cup of this tea each day during the first few months of pregnancy can provide folic acid, iron and copper salts, plus vitamin A and C in good proportion. Raspberry leaf tea can often remove the tendency towards morning sickness.

During the last few months of pregnancy, raspberry leaf tea tones and strengthens the pelvic muscles and ligaments to help with an easy, normal birth. Should a rash appear around your pregnant middle, you could be taking too much of this herb tea! Curb your enthusiasm and reduce the number of cups you drink each day.

Raspberry leaf tea can also help overcome prolapse of the uterus in older women or in those who have a structurally tired uterus from childbearing traumas. This tea has an affinity for the ligaments which support the uterus, tightening, toning and strengthening them.

Other than for its pleasant taste, this herb tea offers little value to males—it is, therapeutically, a ladies' beverage.

RED CLOVER

(Trifolium praetense)

Sometimes known as "wild clover," this plant is commonly found in meadows and fields throughout many of the world's temperate countries. It is a perennial, with deep red flowers (although sometimes they appear paler and in some varieties are even whitish). It is the clusters of small flowers of the deep crimson type from which the herb tea can be brewed.

The strong, metallic flavor of red clover tea results from its high concentration of iron and copper salts. These minerals make it a vital blood tonic, as well as being an important blood cleanser. Red clover tea can improve the blood's hemoglobin levels and the size and number of blood platelets. It can be a helpful tonic for a spleen which is below par.

Taken in medicinal strength of tincture or extract, red clover can be a powerful herb, exerting a positive effect on certain toxic symptoms. For this reason, it has long been used in clinical treatment where cysts of various types have been diagnosed. However, as a herb tea it is much gentler and more suitable for regular inner cleansing. It can be taken each day, over a period of several weeks, to cleanse the female reproductive system. I would recommend this course of tea no more than twice a year, or an occasional cup, as desired, between your other favorite herb teas.

ROSEHIPS

(Rosa canina)

For availability, economy and taste, rosehips tea has to top the bill! It ruby-red color and its berry-like aroma make it sensually refreshing taken either hot or cold. As a winter drink, served piping hot with a wedge of lemon and a pinch of ground cloves or cinnamon, it is stimulating and restorative. In summer the cold tea can be diluted and served with peppermint leaves, lemon and ice. Really refreshing!

The hips from the Australian variety of the

dog rose (*Rosa rubiginosa*) can also be successfully used to make tea.

Iron and copper compounds are found in rosehips
tea, together with a type of vitamin C which
actually *needs* the heat of water just off the boil
to free it from its resin-clad molecular bond. There
is plenty of this vitamin available from one cup
of rosehips tea, enough to make its daily use a
good supplementary source of vitamin C.

As rosehips is technically a berry-type fruit,
vitamins P and K are also found in it. These help
to maintain blood quality and normal viscosity,
as well as providing a general circulatory tonic.
Rosehips tea can replace that habitual cup of
coffee as a stimulant for adrenal glands in a
mid-morning or mid-afternoon tea break. Many
people find that their need for many cups of
coffee daily drops quite remarkably when rosehips
tea is drunk regularly. Indeed, rosehips tea is a
good herb tea to try as a pleasant introduction to
the huge range of teas to be investigated. It can
be sipped by young and old alike, especially during
a cold or a viral infection, but because of its
adrenal stimulus it is not such a good tea for
late-night use. Serve it as a pick-me-up during
daytime energy slumps.

ROSEMARY

(Rosemarinus officinalis)

Have you ever wondered why rosemary is the

plant—symbol for remembrance? A better name for it would be "the memory herb." Rosemary stimulates brain function through its strongly aromatic oils, which penetrate directly to the brain's memory-stimulus cells. As with lemon balm, rosemary will be of little use to you drunk only on the eve of an examination. The secret is to drink it regularly for months beforehand, to stimulate comprehension and memory recall.

Many people are familiar with the dark green opposite leaves of the rosemary shrub. Its woody upright bushy stems and leaves enable it to withstand a vast variety of climatic conditions. This makes it a favorite of home herb-growers.

Restrain yourself with rosemary! If you pick it as often as you want to use its leaves, you will not have any rosemary bush left to admire before long. Buy some dried rosemary leaves for tea brewing, and pick fresh leaves from your bush on special occasions.

Rosemary tea is a cheerful drink, ideal after a hard day of outdoor muscular activity. Drink it after gardening or exercise because it is an effective muscle-relaxant, acting through the sympathetic nervous system.

Here is another excellent use for rosemary: after brewing your tea, tip all the residue from the teapot into your bathwater to relax muscles which might protest after a strenuous day of hard work or exercise.

On that special culinary occasion, the added touch of fresh rosemary is piquant and appetizing. Add dried or fresh rosemary leaves to steaming vegetables, exotic casseroles or slow-cooking meats. This is a favorite flavor of Mediterranean chefs, in whose part of the world rosemary is indigenous. Add rosemary leaves to chicken-in-a-frypan, or to egg dishes.

You will find it easy and enjoyable to become a rosemary fan, for the relaxing properties of this special herb can be used in many ways.

SAGE

(Salvia officinalis)

With rosemary as the memory tonic and muscle relaxant of the body, sage is a close working partner, for it acts directly through the tissues of the brain and the eye to support memory clarity by strengthening the thinking processes. If there is to be any hope of your achieving the wisdom of Solomon, sage tea could be your salvation.

The therapeutic action of sage in the body is often overlooked. For too long it has been relegated to the kitchen when actually it has greater effectiveness in the study or living room. As a seasoning to mix with marjoram or thyme, sage is well known in stuffing mixtures for poultry and game, but do not overlook it as a valuable aid to mental alertness, especially to prolong such faculties in old age.

None of us can retard the inevitability of accumulating years, but we do not have to equate added years with declining mental processes. Indeed, the reverse should apply—and sage tea can materially assist in ensuring that it does.

The more a person is engaged in intensive mental activity, the more benefit will be derived from converting one's beverage choice to sage tea. This tea is most beneficial when brewed from the *dried* leaves because when dried they increase in strength and potency. Its aromatic oils and strong resinous substances become even more strongly active in bodily tissue.

While the Scottish custom of eating sage leaves on bread and butter as between-meal snacks would have some relation to the ready availability of the plant from the backyard, it has perhaps contributed to the reputation of Scottish heads for accumulating a notable degree of wisdom. The Chinese also used sage in the same way—to increase the ability of the brain in its perceptive and receptive learning processes. As an everyday beverage, the ancient Chinese often preferred sage to what we now know as "China tea."

The regular drinking of sage tea is unnecessary if you are a vital, alert and "with it" eighty-year-old who is looking forward to the future and searching for a large home near a school! But if you are a listless, discontented eighteen-year-old, then a few cups of sage tea each day may help dust away those cerebral layers of lethargy and apathy.

For students who are studying intensely, the drinking of sage tea throughout their academic year can be subtly supportive as a brain nourisher. But, as with lemon balm and rosemary teas, a cup half an hour before the examination is going to do you no more good than to assist with urination!

Sage should be regarded as "the wise person's tea" or "the thinker's tea." No matter what your age, sage's brain-supportive properties can be beneficial. Too many Westerners use old age as an excuse, often when they are still in their thirties.

SARSAPARILLA

(Smilax officinalis)

Many sarsaparillas have medicinal uses, but the Jamaican variety is herbally the best. It is a tropical perennial plant which throws out vine-like branches, the tendrils of which facilitate climbing and allow its delicate green flowers to blossom over an extensive area.

What a complexity of important therapeutic properties this plant possesses. Its chemical bounty includes valuable hormone stimulants for both men and women. I have prescribed it hundreds of times for both sexes whenever reproductive problems, related to low or inefficient hormonal production or distribution, are apparent. Ladies with heart-rending difficulties trying to fall pregnant, with dry vaginas, pubertal acne, menopausal depression and period change, early aging, adrenal insufficiency, etc, can all benefit from drinking sarsaparilla tea. So, too, can men with low sperm counts or prostate insufficiency, or with any symptoms related to hormone imbalance, benefit from sarsaparilla tea as part of their treatment.

It is important to note here that I would not advise the drinking of sarsaparilla tea as the only or complete therapy for such conditions thus far described. Rather should it be supportive of the primary treatment—dietary and/or therapeutic adjustment.

For many people, sarsaparilla tea induces quite a laxative effect. For this reason, it should rarely be drunk as an everyday therapeutic aid. Two to four times a week will usually provide best support for the body's efforts to balance its hormone production and distribution.

SASSAFRAS

(Sassafras officinale)

This herb is incorporated into many herb tea blends for laxative use. It is also widely used in many herbal laxative mixtures.

Sassafras is an unusual herb tea because it is made from the bark of a tall tree. This rough, greyish bark has been peeled from the native sassafras trees of North America for countless centuries by the American Indians, who have long been aware of its laxative properties. Some Indians still brew the occasional cup of sassafras tea to keep themselves regular.

In practice, we find the laxative properties of sassafras derive from its strong resins and oils. These are valuable in assisting to overcome the *dryness* of many Western bowels, often the key to their sluggishness. But care should be taken in the frequency with which sassafras tea is consumed, for these resins and oils tend to remain in the bowel for long periods and can actually overdo their job by becoming sources of irritation.

The lack of natural lubrication and inadequate fibrous residues in the bowel are frequent causes of straining to move one's bowels. This may contribute toward the formation of bowel fissures and hemorrhoids. Sassafras tea, if mildly brewed and drunk occasionally, can be gently supportive in restoring the natural peristaltic movement of the lower intestine, re-establishing easier bowel habits.

The laxative properties of sassafras tea are, in my professional experience, of more desirable benefit when balanced with a blend of other teas with laxative properties, such as licorice and/or senna. This will allow a broader laxative effect. Even the best therapeutic agents can be overdone. If constipation persists, consult a health practitioner.

Sassafras bark possesses reasonable quantities of iron salts, which are important to the blood because they help to provide rapid oxygen for the body's energy needs. But it is a herb which should be handled carefully and in moderation and used only for its therapeutic laxative effects rather than its mineral properties, which are secondary benefits.

SENNA

(Cassia acutifolia)

Alexandrian Senna

(Cassia marilantica)

American or Wild Senna

Perhaps the oldest laxative in recorded history, senna has two source variations. Alexandrian senna is a small shrub, native to eastern Mediterranean and northern African countries. This yellow-flowering plant grows to some 2 feet in height and is especially well known in Arabic regions. American or wild senna is native to the eastern United States, where it grows wild and reaches a height of up to 5 feet. It has adapted to the richer soils of the region, reflected in its greater stature, but is unaffected in its medicinal properties which remain identical to the Asian variety.

Older civilizations became familiar with the cathartic properties of senna as a means of relieving their bowels following their indulgences in overeating during those occasional times of abundant food. It was also found useful in ridding the bowels of intestinal worms.

Today, senna is used in much the same way as
sassafras. It is most commonly found in herb tea
blends designed for laxative application. The
leaves are dried and mixed together with ground
pods of the senna plant for best therapeutic use.
It is non habit-forming and does not have to be
increased in strength to maintain a firm laxative
effect in cases of stubborn constipation. In chronic
cases it is always best to investigate the causes
of such constipation.

Senna tea is regarded as the safest laxative for
use during pregnancy, if constipation occurs. It
should not gripe or produce contractions in the
abdomen, which could be dangerous for the
mother-to-be.

SLIPPERY ELM BARK

(Ulmus fulva)

Many and varied are the extravagant claims made
for slippery elm bark. Anything from an unwanted
pregnancy to an hiatal hernia has traditionally
had it prescribed. In its powdered form, slippery
elm bark has afforded such beneficial relief for
many people's ulcerous or irritated stomach or
bowel linings that the abatement of pain has led
them to attribute quite imaginative powers to
the powdered bark of the tall, deciduous elm
tree.

In powdered form, slippery elm bark contains

such a high percentage of mucilage that it provides an effective coating of the entire gastrointestinal tract—from the throat to the anus. This soothing film contains valuable calcium salts, plus sugars and starches to support the healing processes of the gastrointestinal tract under its protective cover. But such powerful support is not so available when slippery elm is taken as a beverage.

In the form of an herbal tea, slippery elm offers a very mild application of the pain-relieving, soothing properties of its presence. Similar to marshmallow tea, this tea contains small amounts of mucilaginous properties which, although not sufficient to provide effective coating of badly ulcerated or irritated gastric or intestinal linings, can nevertheless confer sufficient pain relief as to be highly recommended as part of the treatment. This tea is quite safe for home use to drink as often as is reasonably desired, but if any gastrointestinal pain persists or recurs, professional guidance should be obtained.

SPEARMINT

(Mentha viridis)

Spearmint is almost identical to other mints in its action within the body. The dried leaves of this plant, which is common to most gardens throughout the world, infuse into a most palatable herb tea. This is one of the most useful and effective drinks for counteracting flatulence after a large meal and for cooling and refreshing the body in summer.

The cooling and cleansing effect of the taste of spearmint on the tongue might tempt those who fiercely reject the more unusual flavors of other herb teas. It is ideal for finicky palates and especially for children—they relish its crisp flavor.

Apart from its therapeutic benefits, spearmint tea makes a most pleasant drink by itself, or as a base for more elaborate drinks. It can be prepared hot in the morning for a stimulating drink or it can be cooled for a refreshing midday beverage. Its delightful flavor can provide an excellent base for mixing with fruit juices, fruit punches or vegetable juices. It should appeal to children on a hot afternoon after school or after a day of intense sports activities.

As an introductory herb tea, I would strongly recommend spearmint for those non-believers who have not yet taken a voyage of discovery into the new world of herb tea drinking. This is a most palatable means of starting their adventures, by "turning on" to one of nature's most refreshing drinks.

SPEEDWELL

(Veronica officinalis)

Originally native to Europe, speedwell is now

widely found throughout most temperate countries, in meadows and wooded areas. It is quite abundant in eastern United States and in central Europe and Scandinavia, where its employment as a herb tea has the longest history. Hungary and Czechoslovakia are, perhaps, the two most ancient homes of speedwell tea.

Its general therapeutic usefulness makes speedwell tea a popular beverage. One might almost call it an ideal everyday beverage and general tonic. Similar to elder flowers in its herbal properties, speedwell is a mild physical stimulant, although rather non-specific in its action. Its gentle tonic effects make speedwell an excellent alternative to conventional tea drinking.

Containing many organic acids, such as tartaric, citric, acetic and lactic acids, speedwell tea derives its stimulating properties from its effect on the body's nerve and muscular systems. Because of this, it would be wise to suggest that this tea not be drunk in limitless quantities. But then, no tea, herbal or otherwise, should be drunk in limitless quantities; variety is essential.

The rather bland but pleasant taste of speedwell tea allows it to be regarded as a good kitchen standby. Whenever you feel just a little below par, reach for the packet and brew yourself a cup; then allow yourself the privilege of a few moments relaxation in a comfortable chair to enjoy it.

TANSY

(Tanacetum vulgare)

Extreme caution should be exercised in the use of this herb tea. It is, in fact, a very powerful kidney stimulant and should be used only under professional guidance—frequent drinking of tansy tea, if brewed strongly, could be dangerous.

An aromatic perennial herb, tansy is identified by its curious flowers which have the appearance of a yellow daisy with the petals stripped, leaving only the center. The plant is native to temperate Europe and North America, growing to a height of 2-3 feet. The entire plant is harvested, dried and prepared for use as herb tea. It should never be used in its fresh state because its chemical contents are far too powerful for the body.

The Scots have traditionally used a sprig of tansy in the preparation of the haggis because it is a valuable herb for killing parasites that may remain in the lining of sheep's stomach (in which the haggis is prepared).

The application of a powerful herb, such as tansy, should only be undertaken with the direction of a qualified herbal practitioner. Although this remedy is very effective in the treatment of intestinal worms, tansy is so powerful that one could easily become over-enthusiastic in its application, thereby causing possible harm to the kidneys. The high concentration of potassium salts in tansy can cause a definite diuretic effect which is intensified by the presence of the glycoside tanacetin. But in moderation, tansy tea can be quite helpful for some people in assisting kidneys which might be laboring to excrete excess uric acid.

Also present in tansy are organic acids which reinforce its diuretic properties. These acids contribute to the unusual, rather bitter flavor of tansy as a tea. Fortunately, the flavor is often a deterrent to the habitual drinking of tansy tea. Unless your practitioner advises to the contrary, safeguard yourself against the harshness of tansy by drinking it no more than twice a week; and then only if you feel the need for its particular therapeutic properties.

THYME

(Thymus vulgaris)

The common or garden thyme, though well known as a culinary herb, is somewhat unfamiliar in its tea form. Thyme is one of the most powerfully aromatic of all herbs, containing oils and resins which volatilize when subjected to the heat of boiling water. So strongly do they penetrate into nasal and throat cavities on drinking the tea that you might gasp at the breath-catching flavor.

Thyme is one of the most cultivated of all herbs. It is present in many gardens throughout the world, recognized as a tiny shrub, growing only up to a foot in height. It blossoms throughout most of summer with a purplish cluster of tiny flowers. The leaves and the stems are dried for making into thyme tea.

The oil content of the thyme plant varies from 20 to 25 percent. The predominant oil is thymol, which is found useful in a great many household antiseptics. Carracol is another oil present—this is the major oil in caraway seeds. Pinene—an oil present in all members of the pine tree family—is also found in thyme, as is menthol, the refreshing oil found in mints.

With these four strong oils present it is little wonder that thyme has such a powerful aroma. If you find this tea to be too strong, dilute it with a suitable quantity of hot water after the tea is made. Many people find that a 50/50 dilution is the most desirable. But for therapeutic purposes, a stronger concentration will induce the most desirable results.

For sore throats and catarrh of the lower respiratory tract, thyme tea is highly desirable in affording prompt relief. However, if the problem persists, be sure to seek the advice of a qualified practitioner. For singers, teachers and actors, for all who use their voice constantly or powerfully, I do not hesitate to recommend they drink thyme tea. When the vocal cords tire at the end of the day and the throat becomes tense and constricted, making it susceptible to invasion by all manner of bacteria and viruses, thyme tea should be on hand. It is not necessarily recommended for drinking every day, but before and during periods of overuse of the voice, thyme tea can be remarkably supportive.

Slightly diluted thyme tea is also useful as a throat gargle. Whenever you feel hoarse, whenever your throat is sore or irritated, you can find this gargle relieving—use it often at such times.

Do not waste the remains of your thyme tea. The soggy residues make an excellent toilet flush, for the antiseptic oils they contain are powerfully germicidal. They can also be tipped into outside drains and vents to keep them smelling "sweet."

VALERIAN

(Valeriana officinalis)

It is always a difficult choice to determine which herb tea is the best. Although "the best" is different under varying circumstances, it would be hard to overlook valerian's claim to being one of the most *valuable* of all herb teas.

There is almost total agreement on the unpleasantness of the rather fetid odor (someone once likened it to the smell of dirty feet in a stuffy gymnasium) and the taste of valerian tea. This has been known to stop a great many people from using it. But if you are in need of its valuable properties, why continue to crave for only the niceties? Sometimes the medicine is unavoidably slightly unpleasant. Sadly, in practice, I have found many people who refuse to try a small and marginally difficult change, preferring to accept the long-term chronic illnesses which valerian tea might, in the early stages, help to prevent.

Common to northern Europe and northeastern USA, valerian is a wild, perennial plant, the root of which contains its sought-after herbal properties. It prefers a humid climate, where the ground temperature is cool for most of the year. Valerian grows well under these conditions, especially with its roots under a stone.

The odor of dried valerian root is indeed penetrating. It should be stored in tightly stoppered jars, away from foods which are known to absorb odors. The process of drying valerian root is very time-consuming. It can take as long as four years, contributing to its rather high cost. When this drying has been completed, the root is generally regarded as safe for human use, but in its fresh state it can be classified as dangerous to human health. So the process of drying has to be carefully monitored to ensure that all necessary chemical changes have taken place.

As a natural sedative, valerian tea stands on its own, but it is definitely not habit-forming. A cup of valerian tea before bed does three important things: its magnesium phosphate relaxes spasms and cramps in the muscles; its calcium phosphate relaxes the internal organs; its potassium phosphate relaxes general nerves, to release tension throughout the body. A cup of warm valerian tea before bed can bring relaxing sleep, from which one can awaken refreshed. It is also important to note that the quantity of valerian tea does *not* need to be progressively increased to maintain the same tranquilizing effect.

There is only one proviso against its use—if you have recently suffered from liver problems, such as viral infection or hepatitis, your liver could be very sensitive and might cause you to feel nauseous when drinking valerian tea. This can be caused by an increase in bile flow, which valerian can sometimes induce. Do *not* persevere with valerian if the nausea persists.

Many people who suffer from hypertension, cramps, muscular twitching or any other symptom of "up-tightness" receive a mild surprise on drinking their first few cups of valerian tea. After each cupful they feel somewhat listless, a sensation they erroneously interpret as tiredness. This is not so. What they are experiencing, perhaps for the first time, is *genuine relaxation*! As they grow to accept their body's need for occasional daily relaxing, they can monitor such processes without interpreting relaxation as tiredness.

For children who are buzzing about happily and actively, experiencing life in all its wonderment, valerian tea is most certainly not suggested Their ability to express naturally and vigorously during the day should induce them to sleep deeply and relaxed. They should then awaken next morning full of energy. However, if the child is hyperactive and finds it difficult to unwind before bed, a cup of the milder chamomile tea can be a preferred alternative.

For hypertensive adults who cannot sit still for a minute, who wear out their bodies with the intensity of nervous energy dissipated in many directions at once, valerian tea can be a boon. It can be an ally against the processes of premature deterioration and disease due to nervous tension. Even the strongest bodies can break down under the strain of constant over-work.

Remember, valerian is a "medicinal" tea. You will need to experiment a little to discover your most suitable level of application. The concentration of the beverage and the frequency of its partaking will depend on your personal needs. If at all uncertain, seek the advice of a consulting herbalist with clinical experience in prescribing valerian.

WILD STRAWBERRY

(Fragaria vesca)

Properties of the leaves of the wild strawberry are similar in every therapeutic way to those of the raspberry vine. There are also close climatic and horticultural similarities in that both plants prefer the colder northern climates of America, Europe and Asia and have similar growth cycles. Leaves of both plants can be brewed to make tasty and therapeutically beneficial herb teas, but the wild strawberry has some special properties which are important to consider.

Leaves of the wild strawberry plant have been held in high esteem by herbalists for many centuries because of their special affinity to certain parts of the female anatomy. When brewed into an herb tea, these leaves provide important minerals for the strengthening of ligament structures which hold female suspended organs in place in the pelvic region. Especially after too many children, repeated miscarriages or constantly heavy menstrual periods does the uterus tire and drop. Medical treatment for uterine prolapse is often radical surgery, sometimes without recourse to possible natural alternatives. Surgery should be regarded as the last resort, for often a mineral-rich, low-toxicity diet, supported by two or three cups of wild strawberry leaf tea each day, can provide gradual corrective properties.

For the male body, where pelvic ligament weakness has resulted in an inguinal hernia, the same dosage of wild strawberry leaf tea can afford important assistance to the body's healing actions. Such treatments, for both male and female, can be continued almost indefinitely, for this tea has no harmful properties. However, it is important to note that the therapeutic aspects of wild strawberry leaf tea do not prevail if cultivated strawberry leaves are used. In cultivated varieties, most of the nourishment is transferred into the fruit, which makes it a highly desirable addition to any diet.

YARROW

(Achillea millefolium)

Our last tea, made from yarrow leaves, is my personal favorite. Almost any symptoms of illness I might personally experience can be removed by yarrow tea. It is not a panacea for all, although its common names, such as "all-heal" and "soldier's herb" should indicate that it can defend you against many of the slings and arrows of your day-to-day existence.

The habit of growth of yarrow is really delightful. It is a perennial and is found in all sorts of cracks and crevices, meadows and gardens throughout the world. Often known as "milfoil," its pink or white heads of daisy-like clustered flowers in late summer make a most decorative addition to any garden rockery. However, one small gardening problem with yarrow is its tendency to spread and creep, attempting to take over the entire garden with a little too much vigor. You can then dig up some of it as gifts for your friends or for drying to brew into tea. So long as a small piece of root remains in the soil, it will grow again into a flourishing plant.

As a tea, yarrow can be effectively used for those days when you have the feeling that your load seems impossible. I know that many of you will say this happens every day of your life, but this is stretching it rather a little too far. For those days when your load is over-heavy, when your ability to get through the day is going to take every last bit of adrenal energy, endurance, stamina, will-power and down-right cussedness that you possess, fortify yourself with a morning cup of yarrow tea.

The tonic effect of yarrow is indeed powerful. Its composition of iron salts and organic acids is complex, but its effect is observable, even as soon as a few minutes after the first cupful. I regard it as a crutch for temporary support during the period when confidence in one's ability to successfully complete a day's task is low. Here, you can recognize its application to "soldiering on!" You can also realize that its employment should not be a daily affair, otherwise something is amiss with your thinking, your life-style or your organizing ability.

Yarrow tea should be an occasional beverage, taken when the going gets tough. Then, you should not think of it again until the next "impossible" day occurs. Hopefully, you should recognize your need to direct your attention to correcting your life-style or your organizing of it so that these days occur less and less regularly.

Care should be exercised when taking yarrow tea. Some women have missed a menstrual period after drinking yarrow tea for two or three days. Other people have experienced the sensation of a dry mouth after drinking this beverage. Both occurrences reflect its astringent properties. It should be regarded as an occasional "pick-me-up" only.

Exceptions to this rule of moderation apply only to people recuperating from an enervating sickness or for those who have a mammoth task ahead of them. Then, I might suggest yarrow tea as a regular drink over a few weeks. But once the recovery has taken place or the task is accomplished, this beverage should not be needed. It can be especially beneficial to people recovering from severe viral infections or from such debilitating diseases as to keep them incapacitated for a period. Likewise, for anyone with a mountain to climb, a long voyage to sail, a huge job to be completed on time or any other exceptional activity, yarrow tea can provide strong support. But remember it will only support your effort; it will not provide the effort without *you*.

SELECTED REFERENCES
& ADDITIONAL READING

Angier, Bradford. *Field Guide to Medicinal Wild Plants*. Stackpole Books, 1978.

Back, Philippa. *Choosing, Planting & Cultivating Herbs*. Keats Publishing, 1977.

Bellew, Dr. Bernard A., M.D., and Joeva Galaz Bellew. *The Desert Yucca: A New Approach for Health and Arthritis*. Spa City Grafics, Inc., n.d.

Bianchini, Francesco, and Corbetta, Francesco. *Health Plants of the World: Atlas of Medicinal Plants*. Newsweek Books, 1977.

Castleton, Virginia. *Secrets of Natural Beauty*. Keats Publishing, 1972.

Challem, Jack Joseph and Renate Lewin-Challem. *What Herbs Are All About*. Keats Publishing, 1980.

Conway, David. *The Magic of Herbs*. E.P. Dutton, 1973.

Curtin, L.S.M. *Healing Herbs of the Upper Rio Grande*. Southwest Museum of Los Angeles, 1965.

Fielder, Mildred. *Plant Medicine and Folklore*. Winchester Press, 1975.

Fisher, Bonnie. *Way with Herbs Cookbook*. Keats Publishing, 1980.

Ford, Karen Cowan. *Las Yerbas de la Gente: A Study of Hispano-American Medicinal Plants*. Museum of Anthropology, University of Michigan publication #60, 1975.

Fulder, Dr. Stephen. "Ginseng: The Plant That Hides from Man" in *Nursing Mirror,* November 30, 1978.

Genders, Roy. *Growing Herbs as Aromatics.* Keats Publishing, 1977.

Harris, Charles Ben. *The Compleat Herbal.* Larchmont Books, 1972.

———. *Eat the Weeds.* Keats Publishing, 1973.

———. *Ginseng.* Keats Publishing, 1978.

Heinerman, John. *Medical Doctor's Guide to Herbs.* BiWorld Publishers, 1977.

Hill, Ann (editor). *Visual Encyclopedia of Unconventional Medicine.* Crown Publishers, 1979.

Hills, Lawrence D. *Comfrey: Fodder, Food, and Remedy.* Universe Books, 1976.

Kadans, Joseph. *Encyclopedia of Medicinal Herbs.* Parker Publishing, 1970.

Krochmal, Arnold and Connie. *Guide to Medicinal Plants of the United States.* Quadrangle Books, 1973.

Lewis, Walter Hepworth. *Medical Botany.* John Wiley and Sons, 1977.

Lust, John. *The Herb Book.* Bantam, 1974.

Moerman, Daniel. *American Medical Ethnobotany.* Garlant Publishing, 1977.

Moore, Michael. *Medicinal Plants of the Mountain West.* Museum of New Mexico Press, 1979.

Morton, Julia F. *Major Medicinal Plants: Botany, Culture, and Uses.* Charles C. Thomas Publishers, 1977.

Muenscher, Minnie. *Herb Cookbook.* Keats Publishing, 1980.

Null, Gary and Steve. *Herbs for the Seventies.* Robert Speller and Sons, 1972.

Petulengro, Leon. *Herbs, Health & Astrology.* Keats Publishing, 1977.

Robbins, Wilfred, et al. *Ethnobotany of the Tewa.* Bureau of American Ethnology, Bulletin #55, Smithsonian Institution, 1916.

Rose, Jeanne. *The Herbal Body Book*. Grosset and Dunlap, 1976.

Sanderson, Liz. *How to Make Your Own Herbal Cosmetics*. Keats Publishing, 1980.

Schauenberg, Paul, and Paris, Ferdinand. *Guide to Medicinal Plants*. Keats Publishing, 1977.

Seifert, Martin. "Ginseng Research from Behind the Iron Curtain" in *Let's Live,* September 1978.

Siegal, Ronald K., Ph.D. "Ginseng Abuse Syndrome: Problems with the Panacea" in *Journal of the American Medical Association,* April 13, 1979.

Spencer, Mike. "Yucca: New Hope for Arthritis" in *Let's Live,* February 1975.

Thomson, William A.R., M.D. *Herbs That Heal*. Charles Scribner's Sons, 1976.

———. *Medicines from the Earth: A Guide to Healing Plants,* McGraw-Hill, 1978.

Veniga, Louise. *The Ginseng Book*. Big Tree Press, 1973.

Vetal, Paul A. *The Ethnobotany of the Ramah Navaho*. Peabody Museum of Harvard University, 1952.

Vogel, Virgil. *American Indian Medicine*. University of Oklahoma Press, 1970.

Walker, Elizabeth. *Making Things with Herbs*. Keats Publishing, 1977.

Weiner, Michael A. *Earth Medicines, Earth Foods*. Collier Books, 1972.

Whiting, Alfred R. *Ethnobotany of the Hopi*. Museum of Northern Arizona, Bulletin #15, 1939.

Wren, R.C. *Potter's New Encyclopedia of Medicinal Herbs and Preparations*. Harper Colophon Books, 1972.